D0680395

WITHDRAWN
FROM THE RECORDS OF THE
MID-CONTINENT PUBLIC LIBRARY

Advance Praise for
WORK HARD, PRAY HARD

"We need Christian young people who will rise to leadership. Lt. Gen. Rick Lynch's book doesn't just tell young people to be bold—it shows them how to do it. *Work Hard, Pray Hard* is full of real life experiences that show that hard work and fervent prayer are important and are the keys to success. It is also a heart-rending book, showing us the fragility of life and our need for faith. Lt. Gen. Lynch is right on track that with hard work and a strong relationship with God, we can effect change not only in our lives, but also turn our entire Nation around."

—DRAYTON MCLANE, JR., Chairman, McLane Group

"In *Work Hard Pray Hard*, LTG (R) Lynch speaks from the heart, delivering insightful and inspiring guidance. His pursuit of spiritual fitness is laser-focused, and he is a walking example of using faith to persevere through life's unthinkable challenges. At TAPS, we are so grateful for his steadfast support of our efforts to help the families of America's fallen heroes find hope and healing."

—BONNIE CARROLL, President and Founder of Tragedy Assistance Program for Survivors, and 2015 Recipient of the Presidential Medal of Freedom

"Like a breath of fresh air, Rick Lynch opens up his life with great humility and honesty. Taking his readers on his personal journey that included desperately dark days and wonderful silver linings, General Lynch reminds us that we are all leaders—and we are at our best when we allow that leadership to be empowered by the One Who created us, redeemed us, saved us and empowers us to be the soldiers of God we are called to be.

I heartily commend this book for leaders called to lead; and leaders who do not yet know they are! It is a wonderful resource for young and old alike; and reminds us of the great joy there is in working hard and praying hard for the sake of the world for whom our Lord gave His life."

—THE REVEREND DR. RUSSELL LEVENSON, JR., Rector, St. Martin's Episcopal Church, Houston, Texas

"Rick Lynch is an accomplished military leader. He is also a man of great faith. In his first book *Adapt or Die*, he talked about the role of faith in his own leadership experience. In *Work Hard, Pray Hard* he opines that we are all leaders and expands on the opportunities we all enjoy should we care to take advantage. An essential read for anyone of faith, or anyone looking for some."

–Gen Scott Wallace (Retired)

"General Rick Lynch's new book highlights one of his sources of strength: His personal relationship with God. Throughout the book Rick gives the reader detailed insights (thru personal stories and historical and biblical examples) as to how best to strengthen that so very important relationship. Exactly what our nation needs during these difficult times."

–Gary Sinise, Actor and founder of the Gary Sinise Foundation

"*Work Hard, Pray Hard* is a great soldier's story of a stirring faith journey. It's also an illuminating account of how to make faith a living thing with direct application to the trials and opportunities of daily life."

–Andrew J. Bacevich, Professor of history and international relations emeritus, Boston University

"Rick and Sarah have lived much of their lives in and around the crucible of war, experiencing tragedy, heart-break and injustice that would shatter the faith of the strongest. Instead, their faith grew stronger. In *Work Hard, Pray Hard* we witness their faith in action and learn life-transforming lessons that equip us to fight the good fight, grow our personal faith and finish the race."

–Pete Geren, Former US Congressman and Secretary of the Army; President, Sid W. Richardson Foundation

"The sincere and inspiring counsel and wisdom throughout *Work Hard, Pray Hard: The Power of Faith in Action* provide a timeless foundation of insight into the what it means to be not just a true leader, but a Godly leader. I have already found myself returning to portions of the book as a resource in my own vocation, but also as I visit with others. Perhaps one of the most salient quotes that sums up General Lynch's masterful book is, '*With God's help, I was quickly able to overcome my limitations and become the leader I needed to be…*'

General Lynch is a proven leader with a stellar record both on and off the battlefield. In *Work Hard, Pray Hard*, he explores the power of faith in action inspiring readers with a message that stands the test of time."

–Craig Boyan, H-E-B President and COO

"'I humbly come to you, not as a preacher, but a student of faith.' These words launch Rick Lynch's second offering, *Work Hard, Pray Hard*. He bares his soul and shares his story in a way that invites the reader to look at their own values and actions. Rick's personal reflections point to faith in Jesus, service to others and an undying call to see prayer as a foundational element of the abundant life. Lieutenant General Lynch is a Warrior and a man who is not afraid to admit his mistakes, limitations and his belief that it is God who brings the victory. Buy the book and enjoy the journey."

–Chaplain (Colonel) Mike Lembke, US Army (Retired)

"'The Power of Faith in Action' is not just a tagline for this thoughtful spiritual journey. What has touched me personally are the examples of struggle and light. St. John of the Cross wrote about the 'dark night of the soul' and the saving grace of prayer to strengthen, endure and grow. What is remarkable about *Work Hard, Pray Hard* is the intimacy as well as the universality of what is revealed through both the battlefields of combat and life. As a meditation and a song of gratitude, this book shares lessons from dark nights and the power of Divine love."

–Dr. Mary Keller, President and CEO, Military Child Education Coalition

"A thrilling account of a powerful spiritual journey. As Rick Lynch recounts in humble transparency his spiritual discoveries and growth, I was drawn into each event and moment of insight as if it was my own. *Work Hard, Pray Hard* is a contemplative view of a child of God finding their place and purpose in creation and in the eyes of God. A must read."

–Ray Bailey, Brigadier General, US Army (Retired), Deputy Chief of Chaplains

"With simplicity, grace and candor, Rick Lynch's *Work Hard, Pray Hard* is a powerful guide—through faith in God—for living with purpose and meaning. By combining lessons learned from a career in the military and beyond with Biblical truths, the retired 3 Star General offers both compelling encouragement and motivation for us all."

–Jim Spaniolo, Former President, University of Texas at Arlington; President and CEO, North Texas Chamber of Commerce

"Through the faith journey of a decorated combat soldier, inspired by the spirit of Captain James Marsh, *Work Hard, Pray Hard* is a roadmap for each of us, and our nation, in our journey toward humility, inner peace and faith."

–FORMER U.S. CONGRESSMAN CHET EDWARDS,
W. R. Poage Distinguished Chair in Public Policy, Baylor University

"An engrossing and enlightening memoir, *Work Hard, Pray Hard* is the very personal account of Lt Gen (ret) Rick Lynch's spiritual journey. Set against the narrative of his remarkable military career, the author introduces himself as a 'student of faith' but by the end proves himself a worthy instructor. Highly recommended!"

–DB SWEENEY, Actor

"Since first meeting Ricky Lynch, my life has not been the same. Rick has taught me that leading by example means living by example. And his simple message about the secret of life—*Work Hard, Pray Hard*—and his inspiring stories about how to live and lead in a world where faith based leadership is all too lacking, will absolutely change your life as well. I'm confident in saying that Rick Lynch has made Captain James Marsh very proud!"

–DOUG HARWARD, President and CEO, Training Industries Inc

"In this book, General Lynch opens up his faith journey to us. He shares the struggles of life and how his faith has grown as he found the inner peace that God desires for all His children. He shares the faith of previous military leaders as well as how his faith guided him and gave him strength to face dangerous situations. Our journey of faith is not easy and General Lynch is transparent about his journey as an encouragement for each of us."

–DAVE JUNG, Senior Pastor, Crown of Life Lutheran Church and School

"Inner peace—if you are looking for the peace that transcends all understanding, start by reading this book. The path is outlined and all it will take is your time and dedication to action. General Lynch tells his story in such an open, honest and interesting way that you feel like you know him and you realize you can find that inner peace—he helps you see it is attainable!"

–SHARON CLARKE, Chief Commercial Officer, Tris Pharmaceuticals

"This testimonial gets 5 Stars for candor, and it reads very well. It is unique in my experience in connecting a Soldier at war and in peace with his God. Tie ins to scripture with specific times and events in Rick Lynch's life are illuminating. This book is NOT about judging others or their faith. It took courage AND faith to write."

–Paul E. Funk, LTG (Retired), EdD, President and CEO,
The National Mounted Warfare Foundation

"Rick Lynch's new book may save your life! Stress can be the kiss of death... Christian faith heals. Each action chapter is grounded in scripture, points you in the right direction, and comes alive with the personal witness of this American centurion."

–James Campbell Quick, Distinguished University Professor, The University of Texas at Arlington, author of *Preventive Stress Management in Organizations*, Second Edition (American Psychological Association)

"*Work Hard, Pray Hard* is a glimpse into Gen. Lynch's journey from passive believer, to active believer, to strong proponent of Christianity. Rick's brutally honest discussion of his personal trial and tribulations is one that every reader can connect with and fill in with their own experiences.

A moving and touching book that should cause all to stop, think and reevaluate their own relationship with God."

–Bob Jansen, President and CEO, Zensights

"*Work Hard, Pray Hard* is the account of this man's life since putting God in control. It's not just stories of how Gen. Lynch lived as he served our country in military service. It is the way he lives his life. This is the story of the man illustrated in fast moving, high action, thrillers paralleled by stories from the Holy Bible that have inspired and encouraged him. In the hours I have spent with Gen. Lynch the words 'God has a plan' or 'God is with us' are part of his daily vocabulary, not just words for this book. He hasn't just written a book; he has lived this book. You will be inspired, encouraged, and challenged to a more purposeful life to be lived not being intimidated by the enemies that attack you, but rather 'standing like a Stone Wall' staring them down to victory then giving God all the glory. A must read for all!"

–Roger Lewis, pastor, LIFEchurch, North Richland Hills, TX

"Reading Rick's books leaves one with a blueprint for living your life, not only purposefully, but with passion and, very importantly, *compassion*, that comes from abiding Faith. I believe that the driving force of his Faith allows him to choose and accomplish great goals, all the while leading with relentless passion, tempered with genuine kindness from within."

–COLEEN BECK, President and CEO, Union State Bank

"It was a great and wise prophet who opined: Four things support the world:

The learning of the wise,
The justice of the great,
The prayers of the good,
The valor of the brave.

In that I have lived and served with LTG Rick Lynch during the lions share of the past 30 years, I can both attest that he has lived his creed, and that he has carried the 'blood-stained banner' to lift, so that God may draw. *Work Hard, Pray Hard* is a brilliant yield by a phenomenal leader, trainer, mentor, and ambassador for Christ."

–BARRYE L. PRICE, Ph.D., Major General, US Army (Retired)

"Rick has an uncanny storytelling ability that allows the reader to relate to him on a personal level and grasp the essence of what is truly important in life. His experience and wisdom come through in his words. This powerful and insightful collection of questions and lessons will guide the reader to improved professional and personal success!"

–JORGEN PEDERSEN, President and CEO, RE2

"The power of putting God first in our lives and then living out our faith walk daily can be challenging. *Work Hard, Pray Hard: The Power of Faith in Action* provides a real world framework that will bring you closer to God and will equip you to be the Leader God has called you to be. The book is both instructional and inspiring! It's a must read…"

–JOHN ARENA, Vice President and General Manager, US Psychiatry, Lundbeck

"As you work hard to execute your life, there are all these questions, doubts and opinions about any journey you may have with God. Why it matters?, how to start?, why continue?, how I'm doing?... Rick Lynch shares his journey through the eyes and mind of a Lieutenant General, a father, a husband and a friend. As he shares his direct application of unique thought and reason, you will gain valuable guidance and indeed your journey may become a bit quicker, as mine has. He has been through it all!"

—TROY TAKACH, President & CEO, Kairos Autonomi

"*Work Hard, Pray Hard* is a wonderful account how God wants all of us to do just that. This books inspires us all to follow faith with works. The bible teaches us all 'faith without works is dead.' This book shares stories of just how that works!"

—DAN WALLRATH, Founder/President, Operation Finally Home

Work Hard Pray Hard

The Power of Faith in Action

★ ★ ★

LT GEN (RET) RICK LYNCH

WITH Mark Dagostino

A SAVIO REPUBLIC BOOK

Work Hard, Pray Hard:
The Power of Faith in Action
© 2017 by Lt. Gen. (Ret.) Rick Lynch
All Rights Reserved

ISBN: 978-1-68261-256-9
ISBN (eBook): 978-1-68261-257-6

Excerpts are from THE HOLY BIBLE, NEW INTERNATIONAL VERSION®, NIV® Copyright © 1973, 1978, 1984, 2011 by Biblica, Inc.™ Used by permission. All rights reserved worldwide.

No part of this book may be reproduced, stored in a retrieval system, or transmitted by any means without the written permission of the author and publisher.

Cover Design by Quincy Avilio
Interior Design and Composition, Greg Johnson/Textbook Perfect

Published in the United States of America

To Captain James Marsh—
You touched our lives and will be remembered, always.

Acknowledgments

As I often mention, when it comes to my personal priorities, my relationship with God comes first, followed by my relationship with my Family and friends, and finally my relationship with my profession.

So first I want to thank God for all he has done for me personally, and for my Family and friends. I pray the prayer of Jabez daily, and God always blesses me, enlarges my territory, protects me from evil, and keeps His hand in everything that I do. I could not do what I do without my relationship with Him.

I want to thank my Family for their love and support over all these years. They have always been the source of my inspiration. Sarah has been at my side for the past thirty-four years and that is indeed a true blessing from God. Our children Susan and Lucas provide us joy everyday, and I am so very proud of the adults they have become. Thanks to David and Erica for being wonderful spouses to our children. We couldn't have picked better. And, thank God and our children for the love of our lives...our grandkids JW, Rex, and Piper. They make us smile, everyday.

I want to thank my great friend, Mark Dagostino. I thank God that He brought Mark into my life five years ago. Mark is an unbelievable professional and a remarkable human being. I have enjoyed working with Mark on this our second book, and look forward to many more projects to come.

I want to thank Nena Madonia and Austin Miller at Savio. You have guided us through each step of this process. I love your enthusiasm and dedication to excellence. You are a true joy to work with.

In writing this book, all of our efforts are aimed at providing something that will help folks through these anxious times. I hope this book accomplishes that. To that end, I want to thank everyone who has helped, and will help, in getting this book into the hands of those folks who need it most.

Take care and God bless.

Contents

INTRODUCTION
Such Great Faith. v

CHAPTER 1
Searching for Inner Peace 1

CHAPTER 2
Overcoming Limitations 27

CHAPTER 3
Commanding Courage 50

CHAPTER 4
Being Humble 70

CHAPTER 5
Growing Beyond One's Sinful Nature 87

CHAPTER 6
Developing Spiritual Fitness 112

CHAPTER 7
Trusting God. 144

Such Great Faith

Captain James Marsh may well be the most enthusiastic, effervescent human being I ever came across.

James was a young lieutenant when I first met him in 1993. I had just assumed command of the 1st Battalion, 8th Cavalry, at Fort Knox, Kentucky, and he stood out to me the moment I met him. He was a commanding presence at 5'11" with dark blonde hair, and I don't think there's a man or woman alive who wouldn't agree he was one heck of a good-looking guy. But that's not what made me take notice of him. It wasn't necessarily his strong work ethic, either. It wasn't even his exemplary tactical and technical competency that made him shine. It was simply the fact that James lit up the room whenever he walked in. Everyone—and I mean *everyone*—loved to be around James Marsh. He had a great sense of humor. He was kind. He was one of those people who lived life to the fullest; who never put off until tomorrow what could be done today. Let's face it, that's just an inspiring kind of guy to be around.

For all of the above-mentioned reasons, he turned out to be the best lieutenant in my battalion. So a few years later, when the Army promoted me and moved me to Fort Hood to take over the 1st Brigade, 4th Infantry Division, I saw to it that James was transferred to my unit and I assigned him to the most critical position of all: Brigade Reconnaissance Troop Commander. As expected, he went from being the best lieutenant in my battalion to becoming the best captain in my brigade.

I know it seems strange for an Army General with more than thirty years of service to go on and on, singling out and singing the praises of one of his soldiers, but there was just something about the guy.

James was at my house all the time, and my wife Sarah and I both came to love him like a son. James regularly attended my spiritual fitness events at Fort Hood—a series of prayer breakfasts and lunches I put together, open to any soldier who wanted to attend. He and I often talked about faith, and more than one of those talks took place over a glass of whiskey.

The only thing that seemed to be missing in his life was a companion to share his journey with—but that didn't last long. One day, James met a certain MP Captain who captured his great big heart. James brought her around to meet me and Sarah, and before we knew it, those two were engaged. In the presence of the love of his life, I watched James go from being one of the most enthusiastic human beings I'd ever met to being the happiest man I'd ever come across too.

Maybe it shouldn't come as a surprise that a man who was living his life that well would wind up giving me a life-changing piece of advice. But it sure surprised me.

At the end of one particular Bible study in 1998, James leaned over to me and said, real serious: "Sir, I think I have this all figured out."

"What do you mean?" I asked him.

"Life," he responded.

"What on Earth are you talking about?"

"In life, we should all work hard, and pray hard," he said. "That's it."

"Say that again," I asked.

"Work hard, pray hard," he said. "That's what we ought to do."

Work Hard, Pray Hard. I had never heard the phrase before. I wasn't sure if he'd read it somewhere, or if he'd come up with it entirely on his own as we sat there, but man, oh, man did that phrase stick with me.

I've kept that phrase in the back of my head ever since, like some sort of mantra, and I know that focusing on those two simple pursuits has helped me stay the course during some pretty tough times. That's why I figured now was as good a time as any for me to share that mantra with you.

The fact is, we live in frightening times. We're a country that's been actively at war for more than fifteen years, against an enemy that keeps growing, and moving, and changing, and striking from all sides, seemingly without end. We live in a global economy that always seems perched on the edge of some new cliff. Our children are texting and "sexting" and trying things we never even heard of, at far too young an age for them—or us—to comprehend. Our citizens and our police officers are clashing with one another, apparently forgetting that we're all on the same side. And the two big political parties in Washington seem to be at war with each other as well. It's hard to know who to trust anymore. It's difficult to find a sense of security. It's a wonder sometimes how most of us go about our lives or get through our workdays without breaking down and succumbing to worry and fear.

We all feel these emotions. Every one of us. No matter how secure and strong others may seem, I guarantee you that every person you can think of wakes up every once in a while, filled with an overwhelming sense of uncertainty and worry for what the future may hold.

I'll also tell you what that future is going to hold: more war, more uncertainty, more struggle and more cause for worry. In the military we call it VUCA: volatile, uncertain, complex, and ambiguous. That's just the way life is. There have been wars and plagues and immense struggles since the beginning of time. There were problems yesterday and there will be new problems tomorrow. To be concerned about it is normal. None of us are alone in that—and I don't just mean to say we're all in this together. What I'm saying is we're not *alone*.

We've got God.

God is on our side. God is here. Our Lord is actively protecting each and every one of us, right now; and for those who seek Him, through hard work and prayer, God is here to give us the courage we need not only to get through another day, but to persevere against any future obstacle—whether it be personal, national, or even global in scale.

James Marsh seemed to know this instinctively.

I didn't. Not at his age, anyway. But I know it now.

For more than half of my life I've strived each and every day to find answers, and to seek the strength I need from our Lord. He has seen me through the fire, in every sense of the word. He has lifted me up when lifting seemed beyond impossible. He has shown me His strength and His almighty wisdom from the battlefields of Iraq to right here in my own home.

In 2013 I wrote a book called *Adapt or Die*. It's a manual filled with battle-tested lessons for leaders. Since its publication, I've been on the road speaking about those lessons, and without fail one of the biggest questions that comes up at every event I do has to do with my faith. There is always somebody who's curious enough to raise a hand and ask where I found the strength to endure some of the things I've endured, all while doing my best to lead others through some of the trying battles that we faced. My answer is simple: It's my faith in God.

Of course, there are plenty of people in the mixed audience of corporate America who don't really care to hear that much about my faith journey, so I don't elaborate on it too much in most of those situations. Yet, inevitably, a few folks will come up to me after my talk is over and want to have a further discussion about the all-important role faith plays not only in leadership, but in life.

That is why I'm writing this book. I figure that folks curious enough to want to know where real strength comes from deserve a full answer. After all, we're all leaders. Every one of us. You're a leader even if you don't think of yourself that way. When I ask the various groups I speak to, "How many of you are leaders?" typically less than 10-percent of the people in the audience raise their hands. I'm always surprised by that, because far more of us are leaders in one way or another. You're a leader in your place of work, or in your town, or right there in your own home. As a father. As a mother. As a teacher (not necessarily in a classroom). Or a preacher (not necessarily in a church). Leaders need strength. And strength comes first and foremost from a strong faith in God.

The proof of God's strength shows up all the time. God's strength is present in the lessons I've learned in my own lifetime. It's also present in the lessons we draw from our shared history, including history drawn directly from the Bible.

In fact, one of the greatest examples of the sort of faith I'm talking about is found in Matthew 8:5-13, in a passage commonly referred to as the "Faith of the Centurion." In this passage, Jesus encounters a centurion, a Roman military leader who was held in the highest regard:

> When Jesus had entered Capernaum, a centurion came to him, asking for help. "Lord," he said, "my servant lies at home paralyzed, suffering terribly."
>
> Jesus said to him, "Shall I come and heal him?"
>
> The centurion replied, "Lord, I do not deserve to have you come under my roof. But just say the word, and my servant will be healed. For I myself am a man under authority, with soldiers under me. I tell this one, 'Go,' and he goes; and that one, 'Come,' and he comes. I say to my servant, 'Do this,' and he does it."
>
> When Jesus heard this, he was amazed and said to those following him, "Truly I tell you, I have not found anyone in Israel with such great faith...."

> Then Jesus said to the centurion, "Go! Let it be done just as you believed it would." And his servant was healed at that moment.

In case you missed it: Jesus encountered a Roman centurion who asked for His help, and in that moment, Jesus noted that He had not found *anyone* with "such great faith" in all of Israel. Why did Jesus say that? What did He mean by it? What is it we're expected to learn from this encounter? What is the lesson?

I'll talk more about that passage later, but for now the biggest takeaway is that this centurion, a man of authority with many soldiers below him, knew for a fact there was always someone above him who had authority over *him*. This centurion, this soldier, this warrior, this leader, recognized that no matter how many were below him, there was always God above him.

The centurion knew that he, like us, was not alone.

He was also smart enough to know that he could not heal his servant. No matter how much power and authority he had, he knew his own limitations. And so, he asked for help from the only one who could provide that help: God Himself.

There have been many "centurions" since, not only in Biblical times, but also in our own American history who have experienced that same sort of strength from their personal faith in God. From our founding fathers to Stonewall Jackson. From General George Patton to any number of names that may not be as familiar to you, but who've fought for our freedom since, including myself. There are many modern-day "centurions" who have a story of faith to share too. The faith of knowing that God is there. Always.

Whether they know the Capt. James Marsh mantra or not, I guarantee you that every one of those leaders works hard and prays hard. Some of our greatest leaders of all types—from local leaders to spiritual leaders to government leaders and military leaders who've led thousands, hundreds of thousands, even millions of people—have recognized that no matter how great their power might be, God's higher power is always present, and it is with Him where the greatest power lies.

I've steeped myself in the histories of Christian soldiers stretching all the way back through every war and crisis we've ever faced in this country, and all the way back to the earliest lessons of the Old Testament. What I've found is that those who came before us offer lessons in the strength of faith that are just as relevant and meaningful today as they were dozens and even hundreds of years ago. It is from those lessons, the very lessons I aim to share in these pages, from which I draw my strength every day. It's taken my entire lifetime to under-stand those lessons. Hopefully by reading this book, you will have a chance to absorb these lessons at a bit of a faster clip than I absorbed them myself.

I wasn't baptized until I was 32 years old. I did not come to my faith lightly, and I did not come without doubts born of my own weakness. I've made plenty of mistakes along the way, too, and just about every time I make a mistake I'm reminded of one particular line from the Bible: "We all have sinned and fall short of the glory of God." (Romans 3:23)

We're not alone in that, either.

Faith takes work. It takes action. In fact, that's laid out pretty clearly in the Bible, too, in James 2:17:

> Faith, by itself, if it is not accompanied by action, is dead.

It's taken me more than thirty years to reach a point where I truly know that God is with me, always, in every minute of every day, in every situation, guiding me and leading me onward. It's a wonderful feeling, a blessed feeling, and one that I hope others will come to in their own time through their own understanding and revelations. But it takes work. (And don't forget the prayer part too.)

Look, I'm not here to convert anybody. I'm not expecting everyone to believe the same way I do. My prayer is that anyone who picks up this book may find some peace in these seven chapters; perhaps a renewed sense of strength and a new understanding of how great faith can allow us to find inner peace and persevere through life's great trials.

If there's one thing I've learned as both an Army General and a soldier of Christ, it's that no matter how difficult life may seem, no matter how much strife and worry we face today, there are others who have been through more, there are others who have been through worse, and there are lessons from history that can help us put everything we're going through— no matter what it might be—into perspective. I'll share some of those lessons in the pages that follow. I've steeped myself in those lessons, going back to my days as a cadet at West Point, long before I came to Christ, straight through my time on the ground in Kosovo and the Middle East, and continuing through the everyday lessons I'm still learning today.

Which brings me to one last point I'd like to make before you launch into the rest of this book. Every so often after I speak in a church or in front of a Bible study group, someone will ask me: "Has your faith ever been tested?"

I can't help but smile a bit at the sheer irony of the question. "Yes, ma'am," I'll say. "My faith has been tested more than I care to recall!" For one, my faith was tested each and every time I lost one of my soldiers in combat. During the 2007 surge in Iraq, 153 young Americans lost their lives under my command. That's 152 sons, brothers, fathers, uncles, nephews—and one daughter—all of whom were entrusted to my care as they served our country in the toughest ground-war we've seen since Vietnam. I have a collection of baseball-card-sized photographs of each and every one of those soldiers. I take that stack of cards with me wherever I travel. When I'm at home, I keep them on my desk and look at them every day, so their names and faces and sacrifices will never be forgotten—and every day I ask God why they had to die.

I've seen my faith tested in smaller ways, too, when dealing with the ups and downs of life, of work, of raising my children, and in watching the ups and downs of the leadership in this country while wondering where our priorities have gone.

Sometimes, it's hard not to question what God is thinking. There were even times in my past, when faced with the cruelties of life itself, when I questioned whether God existed at all.

In fact, it was just two months after Capt. James Marsh put his "Work Hard, Pray Hard" mantra in my ear when my faith endured one of its greatest tests, ever.

I was out cleaning my garage, doing some work and thinking about taking my Harley for a spin on that sunny afternoon, when I got a phone call from the Secretary of the General Staff (SGS).

"Do you have a Capt. Marsh in your brigade?" he asked me.

"Yes, sir, I do," I said. I figured he was calling with some good news. More than once I'd requested that James be recognized for the work he was doing. *Maybe he is finally being recognized*, I thought.

"Well," the SGS said. "Capt. Marsh was just killed in a traffic accident."

I don't think his words could have shocked me more had he told me that my own son had been killed. I fell to my knees, and I started crying.

No, no, no! Not James! No!

Sarah heard me from inside the house and came out to see what was wrong. She couldn't figure out why I was so upset until I finally got the words out, and then she started crying too.

James had been riding in the passenger seat of a vehicle that was involved in a terrible accident. James' fiancée, the love of his life, was driving on wet roads near Fredericksburg, Texas, when she lost control of the vehicle. The vehicle rolled over. James was killed instantly. By some miracle, his fiancée walked away—forever marked by the emotional scar of losing the man she loved, and who loved her right back.

How could this happen? Why would this happen?

It didn't take long for my shock and sadness to turn to anger. I couldn't sleep that night. I walked out to my garage and paced around, asking God: "Why? Why'd you take him? Of all people! Why *him*? Why'd you take him that way, with his fiancé driving? How could you do that to him? To *her*? I don't understand!"

God has yet to give me an answer to those questions, which is why me and God got some talking to do when I see him. Come to think of it, I've got a whole lot of questions I want answers to when my day comes.

Sarah and I accompanied Capt. James Marsh's body back to Indiana, where we stood at his mother's side while she watched her son get put in the ground. I'm still in touch with her to this day, and I'm a proud supporter of the Capt. James Marsh Memorial Scholarship fund she set up in his name at his alma mater, the University of Indiana.

My heart still breaks every time I think about that senseless tragedy. There was no one to blame, no one to punish, no vengeance to be had—none of the things that sometimes fill our human minds with false comfort in the wake of painful circumstances. It was *senseless*, and that tremendous loss made me question everything I thought I knew about the value of faith, and the value of life itself.

So yeah, my faith has been tested. It was tested before, and it's been tested since too. Yet in time, what I realized in the aftermath of the loss of James Marsh was that my faith didn't wane at all. In fact, it grew stronger.

People seem to want to know how that happened. How can a person still have confidence in God when so many good people are taken from us far too soon? How can a person stand up for God, even after praying for the safety and healing of a loved one, and then watching that loved one die?

Finding those answers in my own faith journey have been a long time coming, which is why I've dedicated an entire chapter to the subject of trusting God toward the tail end of this book. But I'll tell you this: God is infinite, and in our limited capacity as human beings we will never know why God does what He does.

What's amazing to me is to now recognize that we don't have to be frustrated by that fact. Instead, we can ask for His healing, ask for His help, and ask for His understanding. What the Bible tells us, and what those who came before us have tried to show us, is that in asking, in praying, in working to be a faithful, respectful, humble person in the presence of God, we will be healed, we will be helped, and we will have the peace of knowing that our faith will comfort us no matter the circumstance. Even when we don't understand it.

It took a lot of hard work and even harder prayer to get me to this point, which is why I humbly come to you not as a preacher, but as a student of faith—one whom I hope can serve as an informative teacher. I believe it is up to Christians to spread the faith however we can. The best way I know how to spread my faith is through example; and by sharing these examples of the power of faith in action from my own life, bolstered by history and backed by the Bible, what I hope you'll find is a strength like no other. A faith that will not leave you. A faith you can trust to see you through the toughest trials and tests of a lifetime.

Imagine just how strong we could be if we all pulled together with that same strength as a nation.

Imagine what would happen if we all worked hard and prayed hard, together.

I know that's a lofty goal, but it's a goal God wants us to pursue. As it says in 2 Chronicles 7:14:

> If my people, who are called by my name, will humble themselves and pray and seek My face and turn from their wicked ways, then I will hear from heaven and forgive their sin and will heal their land.

With God, all things are possible.

Capt. James Marsh lived his life with the Faith of the centurion. It flowed from him in the pure joy and enthusiasm that he shared so easily with others; the joy and enthusiasm that came from an inner peace of knowing that God had his back, always—even in ways we here on Earth cannot possibly understand.

"Work Hard, Pray Hard," James said. That was his secret to life. He wanted me to share in the power of that seemingly simple mantra, and I have.

He wanted you to share in it too. He wanted it for all of us.

That is why I dedicate this book to him, and I hope these pages do him proud.

CHAPTER 1

Searching for Inner Peace

No one expects to wake up to a nightmare on a random Sunday morning. The thing about tragedy, though, is how often it comes without warning.

On May 15, 1988, I got out of bed before the sun was up, as I always did in my Army days, and still do to this day. I didn't have much of a meaningful morning routine back then, but at some point I turned on the TV news, as I often did. I expected to catch the weather report and some sports scores. Instead, to my shock and dismay, the TV lit up with a stream of images that seared into my memory forever: a mangled school bus, flashing red-and-blues, flames reaching into the night sky, men and women holding each other and weeping. The pictures soon gave way to details: a bus full of kids, teenagers mostly, all members of a church group on a field trip to an amusement park. On their way back home, around 11 o'clock at night, a pickup truck came barreling down the highway in the wrong direction and hit that bus, head-on.

The crash happened in Carrollton, Kentucky, but the bus belonged to the Assembly of God Church in Radcliff—the small town located just outside the gates of the Fort Knox military reservation, not more than two miles from where I was standing, in my living room, in shock.

The reports that early Sunday morning suggested the driver of the pickup might have been a drunk driver—a claim that would turn out to be absolutely true—and the details of that crash kept unfolding in a gut-wrenching horror story, the likes of which no one would ever want to imagine.

It turned out none of the sixty-six people on board were killed in the initial impact of the crash itself. No. Their fate was far worse. That old school bus, built in 1976, was powered by gasoline. The force of the crash punctured the gas tank. The sparks that flew from metal scraping on pavement ignited the fuel. The whole bus became engulfed in flames from floor to ceiling within two minutes. There weren't enough emergency exits on that old bus. No pop-out windows. No hatches in the ceiling. The only exit that wasn't blocked was the door in the back—and the center aisle of that bus was only twelve inches wide. While the valiant bus driver tried to extinguish the flames with a fire extinguisher, and some of the bigger kids tried unsuccessfully to kick out windows, and passing motorists stopped and tried desperately to pull passengers from the back, risking their own lives in the name of saving others, the crush of those sixty-six people trying to escape the flames through one small door was too great.

Twenty-seven passengers never made it out. Twenty-seven members of our local community, many of them the sons and daughters of my fellow soldiers at Fort Knox, perished. All at once. All in one horrific night.

It was the third worst bus crash in the history of the United States, and the worst drunk-driving related accident in U.S. history.

My wife, Sarah, and I were not churchgoers back then. We only went to church on special occasions. I didn't have a personal relationship with God, and frankly, with two young children, my military career on a fast-track, and Sarah taking classes at night to get her master's degree in teaching, who had time to go to church? Sunday mornings were the only time in the week when we got a chance to rest, even a little bit.

Yet for some reason, in our stunned disbelief and heartache that Sunday morning, church seemed like the only logical place to go.

We didn't belong to the Assembly of God church where the bus had originated, so we made our way to the nondenominational Protestant chapel on base. We soon found ourselves in a building packed to standing-room-only capacity. It seemed as if all of our Army neighbors who woke up to the news decided church was the best place to go too.

The Carrollton bus crash was without a doubt the most shocking, heartbreaking, disturbing thing I had encountered in my thirty-two years. I remember hugging my kids and Sarah so tight that day. For weeks after it happened I just remember being thankful we were all okay—while feeling so sorry for the families this tragedy had touched directly. I knew the events of that tragedy would ripple for decades to come. Families would crumble in pain. Entire lifetimes would be changed. I couldn't imagine suffering that kind of heartbreak.

What if it were one of my own children? I thought. *I'd never make it.*

The whole thing made me angry, too: *Why hadn't somebody stopped that drunk from getting into his car? Why the heck weren't there more emergency exits on the bus? What in God's name was a bus full of children doing on the highway that late at night anyway? There are people to blame for this tragedy, and those people need to pay!* I thought.

I was even angry at God. I remember walking out of the church that Sunday wondering why anyone bothered to go to church: *How in the heck can people believe in a God that would let something like this happen?*

Like I said, I didn't have a personal relationship with God back then, and I'm guessing I wasn't the only one who felt angry. I'm pretty sure a whole lot of people questioned God and even questioned God's *existence* in the wake of that accident.

For a moment in time, the horror of the Carrollton bus crash touched an entire nation. And then, as it always does, the nation moved on. There would be lawsuits. There would be changes made to bus safety codes. There would be new cries to stop the ravages of drunk drivers on our roads. But no matter what anyone did, no matter what laws were changed and what good might come out of the lessons learned from that awfulness, not one of those parents would ever get their child back. Not one person who was directly involved would ever go another day in their lives without thinking of that horrible night. Not one person who experienced any part of it would ever get over waking up Sunday morning to something they never imagined could happen—not in *their* state, in *their* city, in *their* town, to *their* neighbors, to them, to their loved ones, or to anyone they actually knew.

That summer, the Army promoted me early to the rank of Major. They transferred me to Command and General Staff College at Fort Leavenworth, Kansas. To be perfectly honest, a small part of me was glad to get away from Fort Knox. Sarah and I did all we could to hold back the tears each time we drove past the countless prayers and good thoughts that were hung on colored poster board in just about every shop window in Radcliff. I was glad to get away from the sadness that would linger there for a long, long time. I didn't want to be around that kind of pain, and I didn't want my kids to be around it, either. I know that may sound terrible. It wasn't that I didn't feel empathy for those around me. It's more that I felt so much empathy that I didn't know how to process it all.

How can any person be expected to go on about their business and get on with their lives after something so tragic occurs? How is anyone supposed to deal with that sort of pain? How do we come to grips with it?

Frankly, back then, it seemed to be a whole lot easier just to walk away.

Chaos Factor

Walking away isn't nearly as easy as it sounds, of course. Even if I was walking away, physically, I couldn't seem to escape the anxiety and fear—not only of unforeseen circumstances and tragedies that might befall any one of my loved ones at any moment, but also of the everyday stress and worry that seemed to keep coming my way. In my early thirties, it felt as if *everything* in my life was perched on the edge of a cliff, at all times. It was pure anxiety. Everything was hard. I seemed to worry all the time, and the pressure never seemed to let up.

Sarah and I were both highly motivated, strong-willed people. When we first went to pre-marital counseling, the chaplain told us not to go through with it. He thought we were too diametrically opposed to each other to ever make a marriage work, and in those days of stretched finances and new babies, I think we both had a few moments where we wondered if he might have been right.

When we moved to Fort Knox, it was right after I'd earned my master's degree at MIT. The Army had sent me to that prestigious school to learn about robotics, and for the first time in my life I spent every day feeling like I was the dumbest kid in class. I'd been a high-achieving, nearly straight A student ever since I entered the Academy, yet at MIT—going back to school after seven years spent away from academia—the highest I managed to score on any test was a 52. I spent two full years studying nonstop, feeling beaten down by the professional students and PhD candidates all around me, and ready to quit every day. Thankfully Sarah was there to keep encouraging me, because without her, I just might have given up. I don't know how she found the strength to pay that much attention to me while focusing on raising our one-year-old daughter, Susan, and then, toward the end of those two years, giving birth to our second child, Lucas.

When we arrived at Fort Knox, we came with a two-year-old and a six-week-old in tow. We bought a house and gained a mortgage that stretched our finances thinner than we expected. Even though I'd previously been working as an Army engineer, I started work in a whole different branch (the Armor branch) on the heels of my robotics training, which meant I had to work overtime just to catch up to my peers and keep my career on track.

Sarah had to take a full-time job to help pay the mortgage and all the additional expenses that come with raising two babies; she also decided it was time to get her master's degree in teaching. I fully supported her decision. How could I not, after all the support she'd given me? Plus, we both knew that getting her masters would help us financially in the long run. But it was hard. There weren't any internet degrees in those days, so she had no choice but to pursue her degree at night. We were excited when she got into a really great school, the University of Louisville, which was 50 miles away. But that meant a hundred-mile round-trip commute to class, which meant the kids were handed off to me the moment I walked through the door at dinnertime. Sarah would give me a hug and a kiss and hop in her car, and I was usually asleep by the time she got home.

We were coming and going all the time, and never seemed to have a moment to stop and breathe.

Even though there was some hope of emotional relief with the move to Fort Leavenworth, I think anyone who has ever moved with a young family knows how stressful it can be. The move forced Sarah to abandon her full-time job, which had basically just started, and all of that chaos put stress on our marriage, of course. I'm convinced that anyone who tells you they have a stress-free marriage is lying. Marriage is *based* on friction. That's just the nature of the endeavor when two people come together to become a family. Figuring out how to make that friction work for you instead of against you is the trick. You have to constantly ask yourselves, "Are we putting flint to steel to make some spark, or are we just knocking two rocks together?"

At that point, with all of the money issues and the moves, the friction between Sarah and myself was definitely not leading to us sitting around a campfire singing "Kumbaya."

Things weren't all bad, of course. I don't really think we were any worse off than most of our peers, and in many ways, things were going well. Enrolling at Command and General Staff College meant I was once again a full-time student, only this time, instead of trying to catch up on my algebra in classrooms full of people who worked out calculus equations for fun, I was studying the art of warfare with a bunch of Army majors. It was awesome. This is the school where Eisenhower went! And where Patton went! And I was one of a select group of captains who'd been handpicked by the Army for early promotion and enrollment. So there were good things happening in our lives. There were *great* things happening. Sarah completed her master's degree, and we were all in good health—other than the kids constantly going to the doctor's office with ear infections and the sorts of things young kids go through. So really, I shouldn't have been complaining. We were blessed in many ways.

We were blessed and full of stress.

Even with all of the good things that were happening, there were times when it felt like we were out on the open ocean somewhere. I wasn't drowning. I was in a boat. I was glad I had a boat. Having a boat is a whole lot better than not having a boat when you're out on the open sea. But it felt like that boat was rocking all over the place. The waves kept coming, the skies were stormy, my family and I kept getting tossed all over the place, and every time I plugged a hole to keep the water from getting in, it seemed like another leak popped up.

Part of the stress we felt in our early days at Fort Leavenworth was the stress that comes every time the Army moves someone to a new home. Socially speaking, once again, Sarah and I were newbies in a new place. All of us majors at the school were in our early thirties. We all generally had a wife and two young kids. And of course, we all drove vans, because that's what everybody drove in the mid-'80s just to haul your kids around. So for sure we had a lot in common with our new neighbors. We just needed to find a way to get to know them.

Sarah and I soon discovered that nearly all of our peers went to church together on Sunday mornings. So we started going to church on Sunday too. We became what I call "recreational Christians"— we went to church because it was the thing to do.

We didn't think a whole lot about what was being said in that church. We went to a little Protestant church on base, which was a beautiful chapel with stained glass and ornately carved wooden pews, but the denomination wasn't something we even considered. We were there to make friends, and that was about it.

We didn't participate in Bible studies before or after church. We weren't really all that interested in the teachings of the church at all. In fact, when the chaplain was giving his sermons, most of the time my mind just wandered off somewhere. I didn't think he was saying anything I needed to hear.

Then one Sunday in November of 1988, our chaplain—a man named Joe Miller—started talking about something called "inner peace." He started speaking about how a personal relationship with God could allow you to lessen the anxiety in your life. He spoke about how a relationship with God could help you to become fearless—and he wasn't just talking about fear in combat or something else related to our military careers, but instead how any one of us could stop fearing that we weren't going to be able to make the house payment, or weren't going to make our grades in school.

He based his sermon on Philippians 4:6-7:

> Do not be anxious about anything, but in everything, with prayer and petition, with thanksgiving, present your requests to God. And the peace of God, which transcends all understanding, will guard your hearts and your minds in Christ Jesus.

Over the course of his hour-long sermon, Joe Miller parsed that passage out. He underscored the idea that every one of us in that chapel was probably anxious about something, and then he reiterated: "The Bible tells us, 'Don't be anxious about *anything*.'"

That caught my attention. *How could a person not be anxious about anything?*

He tried to explain what the Bible said we ought to do: "Just lay it all on God," he said. Through prayer, any one of us could say, "God, here's what I'm dealing with: we're struggling with the finances, we're struggling with the classwork, we're struggling with the kids," whatever your struggles might be.

"Present your requests to God," he said, "and then the peace of God, which transcends all understanding, will be with you." It seemed a little too simple to believe. Was this Joe Miller telling me that if I prayed to God about the things that made me anxious then that anxiety would up and go away? Come on. When something sounds too good to be true, it usually is. I felt I was at least smart enough to know that.

But he kept repeating it from different angles, talking about how, through prayer and petition, God would take care of us and give us that thing he called "inner peace." God wouldn't necessarily step in and solve all of your problems, he said. In fact, you wouldn't really be sure why you changed, or why you stopped being anxious. It would just happen. There wasn't a mathematical equation that caused the feeling of peace. It certainly wasn't because all of the stress went away. It wasn't a matter of A plus B equals C. I was a member of the Engineer Branch who'd gone to MIT. I liked A plus B equals C in my life—but for some reason, on that November Sunday morning, I was willing to let the comfort of mathematics go. The idea that "inner peace" could just sort of magically happen through prayer and petition intrigued me.

It intrigued Sarah too.

As we made our way back from the chapel to our home, Sarah and I couldn't stop talking about that sermon. This idea of "inner peace" felt like exactly what was missing from our lives, and exactly what we needed to find. The constant friction and turmoil was driving us both nuts, and we needed some *peace*.

I decided to go see Joe Miller in person the very next day.

Wading in the Water

Sitting in front of Joe Miller, telling him about everything that had been going on in my life, listing all of the various pressures I'd felt that triggered the constant state of stress and anxiety—especially in the aftermath of the Carrollton bus crash—it became clearer than ever to me that I was doing the right thing. Sometimes in life we're so consumed by things that we aren't even aware of what it is that's consuming us. But after listing all of those stresses back-to-back, I realized I was there with good reason. I definitely needed help. My family needed help. And Joe Miller was ready and willing to assist us.

More specifically, what Joe Miller was ready and willing to do was to "lead me to Christ."

That's a common phrase for what I was about to go through, but to me, it isn't the ideal phrase, because somewhere deep down, I think I already recognized Christ. I think I was a Christian all along. I just never really *knew* Christ. I never really made it a point to relate to Christ. I'm sure if I looked back over the course of my entire life I could find times when I said some prayers, sporadically, and I'm sure there were times when Sarah and I had asked God for assistance together too. Sarah was baptized and had gone to church with her mother when she was young, unlike myself, but in our marriage, the idea of praying together was definitely not a dedicated, conscious act.

Still, I was pretty sure that I'd always believed in God. On some level. Even if I didn't really acknowledge it, deep down, it was there. It was in me.

So maybe the correct phrase is that Joe Miller led me toward developing my "spiritual fitness"—in order to develop a personal relationship with God.

Joe was a slender guy in his mid-40s, a lieutenant colonel in the Army at that time, and in weekly sessions over the course of the next six weeks, he led Sarah and me on our Christian walk. He had us study the Bible. He listened to us talk about our life, and then led us to passages in the Bible that resonated with so much of what we were feeling. For example, as we described the turmoil we felt during our time at Fort Knox, he pointed us to Matthew 8:23-26:

> Then he got into the boat and his disciples followed him. Suddenly a furious storm came upon the lake, so that the waves swept over the boat. But Jesus was sleeping. The disciples went and woke him, saying, "Lord, save us! We're going to drown!"
>
> He replied, "You of little faith, why are you so afraid?" Then he got up and rebuked the winds and the waves, and it was completely calm.

13

God calmed the waters. With a faith in Jesus, Joe Miller explained, we could fall asleep peacefully on the boat, no matter how rocky the seas—knowing we were safe in God's hands.

I know I sound a bit naïve here, but it was absolutely remarkable to me to think that there were passages in the Bible—this ancient book, which I had never read, which I had never even cared to open—that seemed as if they were written directly for me, addressing the feelings I was encountering and the difficulties I was experiencing in my life.

I was nervous, though. What if it was too late for me to find the sort of faith in God that Joe Miller was trying to show me? What if I was too old, too set in my ways, too skeptical a thinker to accept such a thing?

That's when I was first introduced to the Apostle Paul. This Apostle, a man who wrote fourteen of the twenty-seven books of the New Testament, had not only rejected Christianity for the first half of his life, he had actually spent many of those years persecuting Christians. But then, at the age of 32—the same age I was at that very moment—Paul encountered the resurrected Jesus on the road to Damascus. He was converted and he spent the next thirty years of his life preaching the Gospel of Jesus.

That certainly seemed like an encouraging coincidence.

I also discovered that Jesus himself was not baptized until he was thirty years old. I didn't understand why Jesus had to be baptized, since he was the son of God, but the fact that even Jesus wasn't baptized as an infant gave me some additional assurance that it wasn't too late for me to do this thing.

Still, I worried. I worried that there was too much to learn. I worried that my lack of Christian upbringing left me so far behind the curve that I might fail—the way I failed on assignments and exams during my time at MIT. I didn't want to feel that sort of humiliation again.

But Joe Miller assured me that my lack of knowledge was not an obstacle to my success in God's eyes. Far from it. It was a strength, he told me, because I was now so hungry to learn, so hungry for God's help, so willing to put in the work it would take to discover my true faith.

He pointed me to James 1:2-5:

> Consider it pure joy, my brothers and sisters, whenever you face trials of many kinds, because you know that the testing of your faith produces perseverance.
>
> Let perseverance finish its work so that you may be mature and complete, not lacking anything. If any of you lacks wisdom, you should ask God, who gives generously to all without finding fault, and it will be given to you.

That passage, and Joe Miller's words, resonated with me. The notion of turning obstacles into opportunities was a leadership principle I had already put into action in my career.

Joe insisted I still had a lot of work ahead of me. I would need to continue to study the Bible if I wanted to find inner peace. I would need to learn to put my faith in God, in every circumstance, and to learn how to pray—not just when I was in crisis or when I thought I needed something, but as often as possible in my daily life. I would need to turn away from sin, and—in my naïveté—I was pretty sure I'd been doing that already, ever since I'd met Sarah and settled down.

By the end of those six weeks, I was absolutely stunned at how far I'd come. I wasn't just reading the Bible; I believed that what I read in the Bible was *true*. I did my research and saw how many of those stories were backed by history. The events in the Bible were supported by so many witnesses and supported by so many millions of people for so many hundreds of years that there was just no way it could *not* be true.

I also knew I believed in God. I began to recognize that I really had always believed in God, somewhere deep down, for as long as I could remember.

And I felt absolutely ready to find that "inner peace" about which Joe Miller had so eloquently preached.

After six weeks, I was ready. It was time for me to be baptized.

At that particular church, Joe Miller performed baptisms by immersion. There was a pool up in the front of the chapel that looked a little bit like a spa. It was explained to me that during the ceremony, I would walk right down into that pool of holy water, and my whole body would be plunged into it. I liked the basic idea of that. I figured with all the sin that had accumulated in my previous thirty-two years, immersion was probably a pretty good approach. A little bit of sprinkling on my head probably wasn't going to do the trick.

Much to my delight, Sarah had committed to be baptized as well, at the same time, even though she had already been baptized as a child. We both committed to starting this new journey together, and after six years of marriage, it felt as if we were recommitting to everything we had promised at the start of our life together, and then some.

When the day finally came, I didn't really know what to expect. I'd never been baptized before, and I didn't know if it would hurt. I'm not being flippant here. Given all of the fire and brimstone stuff I'd been steeping myself in through reading the Bible during that very intense six-week training course, I didn't know if there might be some sort of a physical reaction when I stepped into the water—because I was a man of sin. I realize all of us are guilty of sin. As I mentioned in the introduction, the Apostle Paul wrote, "All have sinned and fall short of the glory of God." I was getting to like this Paul character. He seemed like a guy who was willing to be open about his shortfalls. He said in the book of Romans, "Why do I do what I know I'm not supposed to do?" Haven't we all felt that way at one time or another? Like we were doing things we knew were wrong, but we went ahead and did them anyway?

That certainly was an apt description of the way I'd carried myself for much of my life before I met Sarah. I knew I was a man of sin, so I didn't know if when I got into that baptismal font it might start boiling my skin or something. Okay, maybe that's a bit of an exaggeration, but I honestly did feel scared. I loved the idea that I was about to be washed clean in the water, but I'd also come to learn that the only man who hadn't sinned, the only man who was pure in the eyes of God, was Jesus—and look at the fate that had befallen *him*. We humans went ahead and crucified Him on the cross! Could it be that my fate when stepping into that water as a known sinner might be something awful?

With Joe Miller's counseling, and holding steady to Sarah's hand, I stepped down into the water anyway. There was no steam, no boiling bubbles around my toes, so I kept on walking. I followed Joe's instructions and helped lower Sarah down into the water when the time came, and then she helped lower me down at the appropriate time too. We experienced that moment together.

I dried off like you're supposed to dry off after the ceremony. Those in attendance came up and started congratulating us on our baptism. And as we walked out of that chapel hand in hand, I swear to you, something felt different.

It was literally like a load had been lifted off my back.

I no longer felt as burdened as I did before I got baptized.

I had walked into that chapel still stressed and worried; and when I walked out of that chapel baptized, I felt totally different.

I felt that all the burdens I'd been carrying were now lessened.

The burdens were not gone. The bills were still there, and the kids were still being kids, and the tasks I had to do for school were still right in front of me. It wasn't as though I walked out the chapel and into some sort of paradise; I walked out and I was still living at Fort Leavenworth.

I just felt like I could deal with everything in an easier way.

That peace of God, which transcends all understanding: I felt that. I actually felt it. Then and there. Just like that. It made no logical sense to me. A little skeptical voice inside of me, which had been so much a part of me in the past, wondered if I might be losing my mind. But it didn't take much to silent that voice.

I knew what I felt, and I knew it was real.

For the first time in as long as I could remember—maybe for the first time in my entire life—I felt what can only be described in those amazing two words: "inner peace."

Training Days

Was it really that easy? Six weeks, a dip in the baptismal pool, and inner peace was mine?

As an Army man, trained in combat, trained in leadership, I should have known better. Heck, as a human being who'd lived for thirty-two years with his eyes open I should have known better. Great things don't come without hard work and effort. I should have known it just from looking at the work I'd put in trying to achieve a new level of physical fitness.

When I was at Fort Knox, I got on a triathlon kick—not because I felt the need to add something else to my busy plate, but because I thought staying physically fit might help give me the strength to make it through those busy days. So I started doing a lot of exercise and running. The guy who worked with me was a young captain named Michael Gallagher. He and I would run five, six miles at a time, and he was always pulling me along. I certainly wasn't ever pulling him. I was struggling. I felt like I wanted to die on some of those runs. I felt like I wanted to quit. But Michael wouldn't let me. He was in much better running shape than I was; the guy was probably zero percent body fat and seemed to be in perfect condition. The fact that he could do the same runs I was sweatin' and do them with a smile on his face was a pretty good motivator for me. I knew if I kept going, if I put in the hard work, my body would respond and eventually I could get to that point, too. As it was, starting from scratch, Michael helped me get into good enough shape to compete.

Anyway, Michael was married with two kids and feeling a lot of the same pressures we were feeling in the Lynch family during that time period in our lives, and the solution he found to his problems was to opt to get out of the Army. Not long before Sarah and I moved to Fort Leavenworth, Michael transitioned from the military to a wildly promising career down in Greenville, Texas, right outside of Dallas. I was sad to see him go. We were friends. Good enough friends that when we said we'd stay in touch, we actually did. Still, I missed our runs. Without Michael there, I quickly lost my motivation to keep chasing triathlons. I would continue to work out, however. Physical fitness would play an important role in my overall health for the rest of my life. I still make it a mission to do a couple of hours of physical training every day. But I can't tell you how many times I would find myself in the middle of a run, wishing Michael was still around to encourage me to push myself a little bit harder.

About a month after I was baptized, just as everything seemed to be getting a little easier in my life, I got a call from Michael's wife. She sounded real upset, and my heart sunk instantly just from the sound of her voice. She told me Michael had gone out for a quick two-mile run—and he'd suffered a heart attack.

"Well, is he alright? Is he in the hospital? What—"

"No," she said. "Rick.... He's dead."

I may have been a newly baptized Christian, basking in the inner peace of accepting Jesus as my Lord and Savior and putting my trust in God, but that news hit me right in the chest. It made no sense. This guy was in his late 20s, as fit as could be. Running five or six miles a day for him was like walking through the mall to anyone else. How could a two-mile run be the thing in life that did him in?

I was sitting with Sarah at the kitchen table when I got that call, and as soon as I hung up the phone I broke down in tears. All the anxiety and fear of life and the horrible things that can happen to someone you care about at any moment came flooding back. Sarah tried to comfort me. I just couldn't understand it. How could a man who took care of himself that well, who had such a bright future in front of him, who was a good father to his two kids and a good husband to his wife—how could *that* man of all men be taken so young?

Looking back on it as I write this book, I realize that this story closely echoes the story of James Marsh, which didn't unfold until a whole decade later. Clearly there were lessons to be learned in the way I handle grief and loss; lessons I wouldn't come to grips with for many years.

But the death of Michael Gallagher was the first death I experienced after being baptized—and it caused me to question everything. Again.

Only this time, I wasn't alone.

I picked up the phone and I called Joe Miller, hoping to get some answers. But no one, not even Joe, seemed to have answers to my questions about how and why something like his had happened. Instead, he offered his condolences. He said he would pray for the Gallagher family. Then he asked me to open my Bible to 1 Thessalonians 4:13-18:

> Brothers and sisters, we do not want you to be uninformed about those who sleep in death, so that you do not grieve like the rest of mankind, who have no hope. For we believe that Jesus died and rose again, and so we believe that God will bring with Jesus those who have fallen asleep in him. According to the Lord's word, we tell you that we who are still alive, who are left until the coming of the Lord, will certainly not precede those who have fallen asleep. For the Lord himself will come down from heaven, with a loud command, with the voice of the archangel and with the trumpet call of God, and the dead in Christ will rise first. After that, we who are still alive and are left will be caught up together with them in the clouds to meet the Lord in the air. And so we will be with the Lord forever. Therefore encourage one another with these words.

Joe Miller pointed out that in that piece of Scripture, we're told, in plain language, that if you're a believer, you're going to go to heaven. And at some point in time, either Jesus is going to come back and we're all going to go to heaven, or you're going to die and you're going to go to heaven where you'll be reunited with those people you love who preceded you in death.

I found it interesting that the last line said, "Use these words to console each other," and that's exactly what Joe Miller was using those words for on me.

Those words did give me some relief. A little bit. But I really struggled with this idea that I still didn't know why things like this happen. They happen every day. *Every day* you

turn on the TV or open up a newspaper (or look in your Facebook or Twitter feed, which didn't exist back in 1988) and you
see these awful things and you ask yourself, "Why? If God is
good, and God is omnipotent, and God is omniscient, why
would God allow that to happen?"

It bothered me. So I said to Joe Miller, "Thank you. There
is some relief in knowing Michael is going to heaven, and that
I'll see him there when the time comes, but I still can't live
with not having the answers. Where is that inner peace you
were talking about? Because I'm not sensing that. I just don't
feel real good about what happened here."

Once again, he referred me to Scripture. Proverbs 3:5-6:

Trust in the Lord with all your heart
and lean not on your own understanding;
in all your ways submit to him,
and he will make your paths straight.

That's when Joe Miller reminded me about one important
but often overlooked aspect of pursuing the life I had vowed
to live when I stepped my toes into the baptismal pool: I still
had work to do. Being a Christian is hard work, just like marriage is hard work, he said.

Becoming a Christian was easy. *Being* a Christian was
something else.

He pointed me toward the Officer Christian Fellowship
(OCF). There was a major chapter of that fellowship for military officers right there at Fort Leavenworth, and I started
attending their functions. The fellowship was about more than
just prayer and worship. Its mission statement is, "To glorify

God by uniting Christian officers for biblical fellowship and outreach, equipping and encouraging them to minister effectively in the military society."

The idea was that each one of us, as Christians and leaders in the military, should be out there ministering effectively to others—not through our words, but through our actions. As a young leader, I was all about leading by example. I loved and understood the message of that. This was an organization dedicated to *doing*, and slowly but surely I started to get it.

The message I seemed to be learning was that my walk as a Christian had just barely begun. The message was: "Okay, now you're a Christian. You've officially been baptized. But being a Christian is not just about who you are—it's about what you *do*."

That's a message that would come back to me directly later in life, too, from a very influential figure.

As sad as I felt over the death of my friend Michael Gallagher, I noticed that with every ounce of energy we poured into giving ourselves to the endeavors of the OCF, and to studying the Bible, and to going to church every Sunday, the more the anxiety and unease I felt after receiving that awful phone call seemed to diminish. I couldn't put my finger on why it was happening, but that feeling of being adrift on a stormy sea melted away much quicker than it had during trying times in the past.

I realized I was just starting to put all of the pieces together. I read Luke 12:25—

Who of you by worrying can add a single hour to your life?

—and I was astounded by the simple truth of that message. I read Matthew 11:28—

> Come to me, all you who are weary and burdened, and I will give you rest.

—and I believed it, because I had seen that truth first-hand. I had personally felt that "rest" he spoke about the moment I was baptized.

After listening to the words of Joe Miller, I discovered the Biblical story of Joash, the fourth high priest of Solomon's temple, which seemed to explain that faith is not permanent unless you keep working on it. In 2 Kings 12, Joash flourished because he gave all glory to God. Yet in 2 Chronicles 24, he was devastated because he became impressed with his own importance and failed to glorify God.

The message from all of those Biblical sources was clear: If I didn't want to be "devastated," I needed to continuously glorify God. To keep working at it. To never give up. From that point forward, I needed to give all glory to God and all thanks to my family for all good things that came my way.

There was just one problem: I wasn't quite there yet. I wasn't ready to "let go" of my desire for my own understanding, as Proverbs suggested I ought to do. I wanted to see more proof of God's peace and power. I needed to see the reasoning and the explanation behind it all. That's just the kind of person I am—or at least the kind of person I was.

I was willing to put in whatever work it might take to become a good Christian. Hard work was never an issue for me. The idea of it didn't scare me off. But I needed something more to drive me forward. Maybe I needed some more Christian mentors, mirroring the way I'd sought out mentors in my military career. Maybe I needed to study more, or find some contemporary examples of strong Christians I could learn from, too—some folks who were a little more current than the figures I found in those old Bible stories—just to help me get a fuller understanding of what it was I was supposed to do in order to truly feel that "inner peace" at all times.

Of course, once I started thinking that I wasn't getting everything I needed from the Bible alone, it stressed me out. I had heard and read all of this stuff about God "speaking to people," and since He wasn't speaking to me, too, I thought I was doing something wrong. I worried that maybe it was wrong of me to need more proof, or to see something extra. I worried that I was failing in the eyes of God by not believing as fully as I possibly could; by not being 100-percent certain that I could "trust the Lord with all my heart" and "submit to Him in all ways."

Once again, looking back on it, I guess I should have known better. I should have simply paid attention to what the Bible had already warned me in that rhetorical question that Luke asked: "Who of you by worrying can add a single hour to your life?"

Rome wasn't built in a day, as people like to say.

Well, guess what? Building an unbreakable fortress of faith takes time and effort, too.

CHAPTER 2

Overcoming Limitations

There's a famous last line in one of the old *Dirty Harry* movies from the 1970s. After single-handedly taking down a ring of vengeful, crooked cops (led by none other than his commanding officer), "Dirty Harry" Callahan looks toward the camera and says, "A man's got to know his limitations."

A *Dirty Harry* film might seem like a strange place to gain a little life lesson, but there's a reason that line still resonates to this day. The fact is, we've all got our limitations, and as Clint Eastwood so expressively said it in that film, it's good to know what those limitations are.

The thing about limitations, though, is life doesn't care about 'em. If you want to succeed, if you want to persevere, there are times in life when you're going to have to push through whatever limitations you've got and simply rise to the occasion.

There are plenty of self-help books on the shelves that will try to teach you how to do that. There are plenty of motivational speeches out there that might fire you up to tackle a challenge that seems beyond your capabilities as well. Reading or listening to those books and speeches doesn't hurt. I've read and listened to lots of them in my lifetime. But, as I would come to find out over the course of the next thirty years of my life, those books and speeches weren't all that necessary. History shows us there has long been a readily available answer to the problem of overcoming limitations, and the answer is this: if we turn to God, He's going to help us with our shortfalls.

The Bible tells us in Mark 10:27:

> Jesus looked at them and said, with man this is impossible, but not with God; all things are possible with God.

That's a pretty remarkable statement. "All things are possible with God." *All things*. The first time I read it I remember thinking, *Really?*

Of course, the Bible is full of examples of God coming to the aid of us humans, and one of the most famous examples happened to one of the Bible's most famous figures: Moses.

In 2014, Hollywood brought Moses back to the minds of many through the release of the movie, *Exodus: Gods and Kings*. I saw that film, and what it lacked in Biblical accuracy it made up for in action—and anything that gets lots of people into a theater to spend a couple of hours thinking about one of the Bible's great figures seems like an awfully good use of millions of Hollywood dollars to me.

What some moviegoers might not realize is that the film was based on one of the books of the Bible, the second book of the Old Testament, known as the Book of Exodus.

In Exodus 3:10, God gave Moses a task. He had seen the suffering of His people in Egypt over the past 400 years, and He told Moses: *So now, go, I am sending you to Pharaoh to bring my people the Israelites out of Egypt.* Moses had no idea why he was being chosen for such a monumental task. He didn't think he was capable of doing such a task. The very next line of that passage reads: *But Moses said to God, "Who am I, that I should go to Pharaoh and bring the Israelites out of Egypt?" And God said, "I will be with you."*

Moses protested further in Exodus 4:10-11, complaining that he didn't have the oratory skills necessary to convince the Israelites, or anyone else for that matter, to follow him anywhere, let alone out of Egypt:

> Moses said to the Lord, "O Lord, I have never been eloquent, neither in the past nor since you have spoken to your servant. I am slow of speech and tongue." The Lord said to him "Who gave man his mouth? Who makes him deaf or mute? Who gives him sight or makes him blind? Is it not I, the Lord? Now go; I will help you speak and teach you what to say."

Well, guess what? God did just what He'd promised. He was with Moses every step of the way, and He turned him into exactly the orator he needed to be. Just as it showed in the movie, just as it says in the Bible, Moses overcame every obstacle that was thrown his way and successfully led the Israelites out of Egypt.

With God's help, Moses overcame his limitations.

That particular Moses story stayed with me long after I read it—mainly because I had plenty of limitations myself, and every time I came face-to-face with my own limitations from my baptism forward, I prayed that God would help me to overcome them, just as he'd helped Moses.

Not that I'm comparing myself to Moses. I certainly don't think I'm one of God's "chosen ones." In fact, as I mentioned in the last chapter, I wondered why all of these folks in the Bible and even some Christians I'd met in real life were able to have conversations directly with God, when I'd never heard Him speak to me at all. (At least, not as far as I knew. I'll touch more on that later.) I just did my best to try to trust what the Bible said about all of us being God's children, and therefore hoped that God might help me get over the hurdles I faced.

What's really strange is that as I look back on my life now, I think God may have been helping me to get over my limitations all along.

I mentioned before that my lack of a Christian upbringing felt like a serious limitation in life. Not being baptized until such a late age made me feel as if I were lagging behind in my Christian Walk compared to a lot of other people. Yet, even when I was a kid, God seemed to be trying to do something about that.

I was born in Hamilton, Ohio, on the 6th of July in 1955. Hamilton was a paper mill town, and pretty much everybody worked at the paper mill, including my parents. Despite the fact that they both held jobs, we never had any money, and in *Adapt or Die*, I spoke about how hard I had to work to overcome that limitation. But the bigger limitation later in life would be the fact that I couldn't remember a single time in our family when we ever talked about God. We never prayed as a family. I can't remember *seeing* a Bible let alone opening a Bible at our house. The one time God tried to step foot into the Lynch household was when a minister showed up at the door, and for some reason dad let him in. That minister sat us down and said, "You and your wife are going to hell because you drink and smoke and cuss. And your kids are going to hell because they've never been baptized," and Dad literally picked him up and threw him out of the house! That was the end of any sort of Christian upbringing in my home.

If it had not been for our neighbors, Walter and Peggy Price, who lived right across the street, I would never have seen the inside of a church.

Walter and Peggy Price had a son named David. David was an only child about the same age as my younger brother, who was two years younger than me, and we all used to play together. Walter and Peggy were strong Christians, and they took a real interest in my brother and me. Somehow they convinced my parents to let them take us to church one Sunday.

It was strange. It was a Lutheran church, and it was unlike any building I had ever stepped foot in. I felt out of place. I didn't understand anything that was being said. I'd never so much as said grace at a family dinner. The only routine experience at our family dinners was watching my dad get mad, and my mom get mad back, until something was thrown.

Frankly, going to church with the Prices wasn't any sort of a religious experience for me. Over the years they took us to church another three or four times, and I wasn't much interested in any of it. But by the time I went off to West Point,

31

I was glad to have had that tiny bit of experience of knowing what it felt like to sit in a chapel.

An interesting thing to note: we lived at 770 Fairhaven Drive; the Prices lived at 777. There's a lot of significance to the number 7 in the Bible, and some might say that the number 777 is a numerical indicator of God Himself. Make of that what you will. Maybe it's just a coincidence. Or maybe God was truly there, right in front of my eyes, right across the street, trying to lead me toward a life of faith from the start.

Either way, it's an interesting address that I never considered significant until much later in life.

And, by the way, I'm not trying to disparage my parents here for not taking us to church. It just wasn't their thing. Mom and dad gave me plenty of other important influences in life, including my work ethic. My dad only had a seventh-grade education, yet he was the guy who would pull out the belt if I got less than straight As—and it was those straight As that allowed me to get into the United States Military Academy right out of high school. To this day, I can still hear the sound of that belt slipping out of his belt-loops.

Getting Schooled

By the time I got to West Point in 1973, attendance at chapel was no longer required by law, but it was still very much a part of the West Point culture. The upper classman had been forced to go to chapel, and they made it very clear that we freshman ought to be going to chapel as well. So I did. Every Sunday.

I didn't take much of what was said in chapel to heart back then, but I did find inspiration in a prayer we were required to memorize: the Cadet Prayer.

O God, our Father, Thou Searcher of human hearts, help us to draw near to Thee in sincerity and truth. May our religion be filled with gladness and may our worship of Thee be natural.

Strengthen and increase our admiration for honest dealing and clean thinking, and suffer not our hatred of hypocrisy and pretense ever to diminish. Encourage us in our endeavor to live above the common level of life. Make us to choose the harder right instead of the easier wrong, and never to be content with a half-truth when the whole can be won. Endow us with courage that is born of loyalty to all that is noble and worthy, that scorns to compromise with vice and injustice and knows no fear when truth and right are in jeopardy. Guard us against flippancy and irreverence in the sacred things of life. Grant us new ties of friendship and new opportunities of service. Kindle our hearts in fellowship with those of a cheerful countenance, and soften our hearts with sympathy for those who sorrow and suffer. Help us to maintain the honor of the Corps untarnished and unsullied and to show forth in our lives the ideals of West Point in doing our duty to Thee and to our Country. All of which we ask in the name of the Great Friend and Master of all.

Amen

The things that stuck out at me from the Cadet Prayer were the ideas of honest dealing and clean thinking. I liked that whole idea of living above the common level of life, choosing the harder right instead of the easier wrong, and always looking for new opportunities of service. Those ideas caught hold and served as a powerful piece of my development, as both a soldier and a human.

That prayer didn't come from the Bible. It wasn't some ancient teaching from a historical figure. In fact, it was written by Chaplain (Col.) Clayton Wheat, who served as chaplain at West Point from 1918 until 1926. That's a downright modern man compared to most Biblical figures. And even though it was called a "prayer," I thought of it as more of a code back then; it just seemed to lay out some good, solid guidelines for life. It wouldn't be until much later in life that I'd see how closely aligned Chaplain Wheat's words were to the teachings of Jesus and the Bible's instructions on how each of us should live our lives in order to honor God's wishes. But without me even knowing it, that prayer helped to lay a foundation upon which I would later be able to build my faith.

There were lots of foundations laid for me at West Point. It was on that beautiful campus, on the banks of the Hudson River, where I first got exposed to military leaders who would inspire me in my career, and later inspire my faith as well. Military leaders such as Robert E. Lee, Stonewall Jackson, and George Patton.

Being at the Academy, at the very same institution so many military leaders had passed through since 1802, put dreams in my head of someday becoming a great military leader myself. And therefore, I asked a lot of questions: "How did these leaders do what they did? What gave them the strength and the foresight to accomplish such great things?"

It came as a surprise to me just how many of the military leaders we seemingly all know by name had one thing in common: a strong faith in God.

Could faith have played some role in their ability to win on the battlefield? I wondered.

At a place like West Point, some of these military leaders are presented almost as some sort of gods themselves. I remember walking into Grant Hall, where all the cadets hung out, and on one side of the hall you had a big picture of Lee, and on the other side you had the big picture of Ulysses S. Grant. They were always there, watching over us from on high. In a way, it was difficult to imagine these men as human beings, with flaws and limitations like the rest of us. That was especially true as an eighteen-year-old kid who'd just moved away from home for the first time. I didn't think I had much in common with such great men at all.

Years later, though, I would dig into the histories of these men in more detail, and discover—much to my relief—that all of them were indeed human. All of them had flaws. All of them were at times unsure of themselves when faced with great challenges. And just about all of them, in acknowledging their own personal limitations, turned to God for help.

My favorite painting, a copy of which now hangs in the office of my home, overlooking my desk, is of the great Civil War General Robert E. Lee. It's entitled "The Christian General," and it's a picture of Lee as a three-star general with a young boy on his lap, holding a Bible.

The average citizen steeped in high school or even college-level education on the Civil War likely has no idea that Robert

E. Lee was a spiritual man. He was very private and he never wrote his memoirs. In all the reading I've done, it's clear that Lee didn't talk much about his faith with his subordinates, or even his own family. And yet, by all accounts, he was very humble, and openly acknowledged he had significant limitations. He read the Bible every day; he purchased and distributed Bibles to his men. He has been quoted as saying that his chief concern was to try and be "a humble and earnest Christian."

While staying within the nondenominational confines of military command, he published an order in 1862 that read: "Habitually all duties except those of inspection will be suspended during Sunday to afford the troops rest and to enable them to attend religious services." And he would routinely join his men as they gathered to pray.

It's clear to me that he trusted God, and he demonstrated that trust in his words and actions. One day, a well-wisher was praising Lee for being such a strong leader, and Lee responded, "I sincerely thank you for that, and I can only say that I am a poor sinner trusting in Christ alone and that I need all the prayers you can offer me."

In that one sentence, General Robert E. Lee, one of the greatest generals in history, shows us that he acknowledged his own limitations. *I'm a poor sinner and I need all the help I can get. Please pray for me.* Reading something like that about a military hero definitely made me feel it was okay to acknowledge my own limitations in life, and to ask for God's help to overcome them.

From Battlefields to the White House

Later in life I read similar words from a different sort of leader: President Harry Truman. Truman was not overtly spiritual. He never attended church. And yet, after Franklin Delano Roosevelt's death, one of the first things he told the media was, "If you pray, pray for me." Truman was then Vice President, faced with the daunting task of taking over the White House in the rocky, globally charged aftermath of World War II.

Truman himself was a World War I veteran, and a man of great strength—but he clearly knew his limitations.

After winning re-election by a slim margin in 1948, he acknowledged his own limitations again during his January 20, 1949, inaugural address. He openly expressed in front of the nation and the world that he was turning to God for help in making him the best leader possible: "Mr. Vice President, Mr. Chief Justice, fellow citizens: I accept with humility the honor which the American people have conferred upon me. I accept it with a resolve to do all that I can for the welfare of this Nation and for the peace of the world.

"In performing the duties of my office, I need the help and the prayers of every one of you," he said. He continued, acknowledging the importance of God in the foundation of our common belief system as United States citizens: "The American people stand firm in the faith which has inspired this Nation from the beginning. We believe that all men have a right to equal justice under law and equal opportunity to share in the common good. We believe that all men have a right to freedom of thought and expression. We believe that all men are created equal because they are created in the image of God.

"From this faith we will not be moved," he said. Then, after denouncing communism and setting out an agenda of bringing shared prosperity through freedom throughout the world, he closed his speech by saying, "With God's help, the future of mankind will be assured in a world of justice, harmony, and peace."

I found it extremely interesting to learn that such diverse leaders as Moses, Robert E. Lee and Harry Truman all did essentially the same thing: when faced with challenges, they humbled themselves, they acknowledged their limitations, and they asked for God's help in achieving the great tasks that lay ahead.

There were plenty of other examples to be found, and I'll speak about a few more of them in the upcoming chapters. But the gist of the lesson I was getting was if I truly wanted to achieve that inner peace I was after, then I, too, needed to acknowledge my limitations and ask for God's help.

After I was baptized, there were numerous times throughout the course of my military career when I was suddenly faced with challenges I thought were insurmountable. And in each case, after analyzing the task at hand and being mindful of my many limitations, I turned to God and asked Him to give me the strength, courage, and wisdom to do whatever was being asked of me. In short, I asked Him to guide me.

I know this sounds uncanny, but I kid you not: In every single case, God came through.

Learning Curves

The first time I recall that happening was shortly after I was baptized, when I received my first assignment out of Fort Leavenworth. As a reminder, I made an uncommon career move prior to becoming a major. I had switched branches in the Army, moving from the Engineer branch to the Armor branch. After ten years' experience as an engineer, I became a major in Armor and was basically starting from scratch around a bunch of guys who'd already spent ten years on that career track. That's a pretty steep learning curve by any measure—to throw yourself up against people with far more experience than you have. To then try to lead those same people, since I was a major, was an even more daunting task.

I had numerous senior military officials, including the well-known, highly decorated Vietnam War Veteran, Brigadier General John C. "Doc" Bahnsen, tell me I was making a huge mistake. "You'll never command a tank battalion because you never commanded a tank company!" they said. They were positive I wouldn't be able to get ahead because I needed to follow the same steps everyone else followed, and *that*, they insisted, could take me ten years of catching up.

With God's help, I set out to prove them wrong.

My first assignment after Fort Leavenworth in Germany, with the 11th Armored Cavalry Regiment under John Abrams (who would retire as a four-star general). Abrams knew I didn't know the first thing about working with tanks, so he put me at the bottom of the totem pole and made me his regimental supply officer. That wasn't exactly the sort of leadership position I was looking for, so I called up one of my mentors and asked if I might be able to get a new assignment, a step or two up the chain.

Be careful what you wish for in life. The next thing I knew, I received a call saying, "You're now the operations officer for 1st Squadron 11th Armored Cavalry Regiment." That wasn't just a step or two. It was a giant leap!

They sent me to the Fulda Gap, on the East-West German border, before The Wall came down. If the Soviet Union was going to invade Western Europe, the Fulda Gap is the spot where they were going to do it. So the Army put a cavalry regiment right there, where we could act as a speed bump to hold the Soviets back if they ever decided to come across. We patrolled that border every day, and through binoculars I could look over at the East Germans looking back at us—much like our soldiers do today at the demilitarized zone (DMZ) in North Korea.

As an Armor Major in the 11th Armored Cavalry Regiment, my platform was the Bradley fighting vehicle—a vehicle I had never been in, and knew nothing about. I didn't know how to take the vehicle's weapons apart. I didn't know how to load its weapons. I didn't know how to do anything, and I was supposed to be the Bradley Commander. The guy in charge.

Following everything I'd learned from the Bible, and everything I'd been told in my early Christian Walk by Joe Miller, I vividly remember getting on my knees first thing every morning and asking God to give me the strength, courage, and wisdom I needed to become the best Armor officer possible.

Thankfully, I had a young sergeant E5 as my gunner who was willing to show me the ropes, and thank goodness I was at the point in my career where I was smart enough to shut up and listen. The sergeant showed me what to do, and the rest of the crew quickly taught me what I needed to know to be successful in firing that particular Bradley.

With God's help, I was quickly able to overcome my limitations and become the leader I needed to be, despite the fact that I'd never fired a Bradley before in my life. I was also in the right place at the right time to be a witness to history: I was right there when the wall came down, when East Germans came pouring into the West in search of the freedom that had eluded them for far too long.

A couple years and promotions later, the same basic thing happened to me all over again. The Army made me commander of 45 M1A1 battle tanks. I'd never fired a tank, but there I was, suddenly a battalion commander. So, once again, I prayed to God to help me overcome my limitation—in this case, once again, my lack of knowledge and experience. And just like I did in the Bradley, I got hold of my crew and they gave me the appropriate training.

That soon led me to some unexpected results.

What I was learning about God is that sometimes, He gives you far more than you ask for. There were bits of the Moses story that seemed to apply here, but in ways I didn't understand. It seemed that when Moses confessed his limitations and put his faith in God to see him through a daunting task, God answered by not only meeting, but by greatly exceeding Moses' expectations. He took Moses further and through greater trials and tribulations than anyone could have imagined. (Go ahead and watch the *Exodus* movie to get a quick sense of it.)

On a smaller scale, that seemed to be what was happening to me pretty much whenever I faced limitations head-on and asked for God's help.

In any tank unit, you have to qualify in your tank every six months. That means you go out on a test course and perform maneuvers and fire at targets to make sure you and your crew know what you're doing. A perfect score on one of those tests is a thousand points, and on my last run as a battalion commander, I was the only one in the battalion who scored a perfect thousand.

So, with God's help, I went from never having been in a tank to landing a perfect score. That meant everything aligned: the targets popped up perfectly, every move was precise, every shot was precise.... It was perfect.

It wasn't all my doing, of course. A tank crew is made up of four people: the tank commander, the gunner, the loader, and the driver, who all work together as a team. So a lot of credit goes to my team. But the most credit, I truly believe, goes to God. He helped me overcome my limitations and then far exceeded what I myself thought I was capable of achieving.

With God, all things are possible.

The more these sorts of thing happened to me, the less time I spent worrying and fretting over the "what-ifs" in my career, the more proof I had that God actually does exactly what the Bible tells us he'll do. And thanks to that, with each passing year I gained a little more of that "inner peace" when it came to my career. I knew that "in prayer and petition" I could reach out and take God's hand. He was there to back me up, and to lift me up to the tasks at hand.

A few years after that, on one of my tours in Iraq, I came as close as I'm likely to get to experiencing a direct portion of the Moses Exodus story for myself. Completely out of the blue, I was tasked with becoming the spokesman for the Multi-National Force. That meant I was ordered to be the guy who would get up in front of the press pool and deal with the media on a daily basis, representing the whole coalition of nations who were there fighting an incredibly compli-cated and tense war. I had no media training. Zero. I'd barely spoken to a reporter at a local newspaper in my entire life, and we were dealing with all the big TV stations and news outlets, including CNN, *The New York Times*—all of the major media outlets a person can think of. More important, I had no inter-est in dealing with any media, period. I saw no point, and I certainly didn't think I had the demeanor or the oratory skills to achieve much of anything in that role, especially since the press seemed to have some sort of axe to grind. All they ever reported on was how awful the war was going, and how much this was all costing in terms of dollars and lost lives. As far as I was concerned, the media stunk.

Remember now, I was in the Army. Unlike someone who hates a new position at their job and has the option to go to HR and complain, or even up and quit, I had zero options. I had to follow orders. Period.

By that point in the mid-2000s, I'd had enough experience asking for God's help to know what I needed to do. Immediately after receiving the order, I went back to my trailer, got on my knees, and prayed. I complained in prayer about all the reasons I didn't think I could do this, and why I didn't want to do it, and how awful I thought it was going to be. Then I asked God to please help—with my public speaking abilities, my overall demeanor and ability to keep my cool in front of the cameras under tough questioning, my ability to run a press conference, period; all of these things that I simply did not know how to do.

Sound familiar? Remember Moses? *"O Lord, I have never been eloquent, neither in the past nor since you have spoken to your servant. I am slow of speech and tongue."*

I prayed to God before and after my very first press briefing, and before and after every briefing after that. I also thanked God fervently for being there with me, both before and after every event. And guess what? They all went just fine.

Sarah was sitting at home watching me on TV, sitting on the edge of her seat. Whenever a reporter asked the same question for the fifth time, she got to thinking, "Oh, no, here we go!" She'd seen me get impatient with anyone who asked repeated questions my whole life. She says to this day that she was amazed at what she saw. I didn't even give any of those reporters the "furrowed brow look" that I apparently give when I'm frustrated by someone's actions.

She was stunned at just how calmly I presented myself on camera.

As it was with Moses—*The Lord said to him "Who gave man his mouth? Who makes him deaf or mute? Who gives him sight or makes him blind? Is it not I, the Lord? Now go; I will help you speak and teach you what to say."*—so it was with me.

Sure, there were hiccups here and there, but overall, I was widely congratulated on helping to put a good face on our war efforts. I managed to come up with new ideas, engaging local press to shine a light on the extraordinary work of soldiers from their hometowns. I was able to get cameras into hospitals we were rebuilding, and other places and situations where we were making real progress and actually beginning to make things better for the long-oppressed people of Iraq—who, it turns out, were not all that different from many Americans. The vast majority of them just wanted to live and work and take care of their families, like the rest of us.

Anyway, I won't go on and on here about the positive things we were able to do in Iraq. I spoke about those efforts—including some of the most daunting efforts—in my last book. And I'll talk more about some of them in the next chapter. The point I want to make is that any success I had in every one of those trying moments in Iraq, and beyond, came down to the very same thing: when things got rough, when I doubted my own abilities, the very first thing I did was pray. The very first thing I did was to ask for God's help.

As Paul says in Philippians 4:13:

> I can do all this through him who gives me strength.

The Rocky Road

I want to step back for just a second. I think it's important to recognize that just because things worked out in the examples I've shared, just because I was able (with God's help) to rise above my limitations, does not mean that everything was a smooth ride. It wasn't all easy sailing. It certainly wasn't time to kick back with a whiskey and a cigar and watch as my life unfolded with ease.

In fact, it was pretty much the opposite.

It seemed every time I asked God for help overcoming my limitations, God answered by giving me more work to do. In some cases, the work was obviously related to the task at hand: the job of learning how to assemble and disassemble the weaponry in the Bradley, for instance; the hard work associated with learning how to lead a tank battalion (after so many higher ups insisted it could never happen given my lack of experience); and so forth. But some of the work that came about when God helped me to overcome my limitations was unexpected, including the added responsibilities that are included when your personal limitations are lifted and no longer hold you back.

Back in the Fulda Gap, after the wall came down, I was doing so well that the regimental commander promoted me to become his executive officer. I was only a major, and typically the executive officer is a Lieutenant Colonel position. He said, "Lynch is doing so well, I really want to elevate him above all these other folks." When I asked him why, he said he "saw something in me."

It was pretty cool to get such a big promotion so quickly. I was excited—until Desert Shield and Desert Storm happened. All of a sudden, it became my task to move the entire 11th Armored Cavalry Regiment from Fulda, Germany, to Doha, Kuwait. It was the job of the executive officer to work with his staff to cover all the logistics and planning for this major move across the globe; to make sure 2,500 individuals moved safely and quickly into the dessert, right at the conclusion of Operation Desert Storm. As a nation, we wanted to have an American presence in Kuwait to make sure Saddam Hussein couldn't come back and take it over again, and my regiment became that presence.

The challenge in the logistics of moving an entire regiment is far greater than any logistical challenge I had ever faced, by far. But we did it. Yet again, with prayer and petition, God helped me rise to the occasion and accomplish that task with the help of great soldiers.

Work hard, pray hard, work hard, pray hard...the harder I worked, the harder I prayed, and the harder I prayed, the harder work I was given. But that harder work was made easier through prayer. And so the cycle went. Time and again. Over and over.

Year after year, despite all sorts of obstacles and even tragedies, the cycle continued. Despite incredible odds, and incredible difficulty, I was able to rise to the occasion, to overcome limitations, again and again, to the point where I pretty much stopped questioning whether I could accomplish anything, as long as I had God's help.

And yet, life is more than simply overcoming our limitations. Overcoming limitations is just one part of the struggle we humans face as we try to make it in life.

As I learned from the Carrollton bus crash, and we've all learned from the increasing numbers of random shootings in this country, or going back to the attack on Pearl Harbor, or the mass terrorism of 9/11, or the daily news reports of car accidents, cranes collapsing on city streets, bridges falling into the water, drownings, plane crashes, and more—on any given day, at any given time, often out of the blue, any one of us may face a task or an event that seems too big to comprehend. At any time, any one of us may face down circumstances so powerful they could buckle us; or confrontations that fill us with fear; or obstacles that require us to look great heartbreak—even our own mortality—dead in the eye.

Where can we find the courage to face those fights, and to fight that fear?

I'm guessing if you've read this far, then you already know the answer I'm bound to give. But if you're anything like me, you also need to see some proof. So here goes.

Not long after our regiment settled into our new role in the Kuwaiti desert, not one, but two of those unexpected tragedies came our way.

As soldiers, when we're at war, we're pretty well prepared for such things. We're a little more on guard than the average citizen on Main Street back home. Yet on this day, all was calm. We weren't under attack. We had enough reconnaissance to know that no attacks were imminent.

It was clear out of the blue, against the shimmering backdrop of an azure blue desert sky, when black smoke began billowing from the motor pool on the outskirts of our encampment.

My commanding officer wasn't there at the time. He was miles and miles away on other business.

That meant I was in charge.

I knew there were vehicles in that motor pool that were packed full of weapons, ammunition, and explosives. I knew that whatever was happening behind the 10-foot tall cement walls of that tightly guarded motor pool was not good. I knew that whatever was going on in there was potentially very dangerous, and that a whole lot of my soldiers' lives were potentially at risk.

I quickly prayed to God to get all of us through whatever crisis was about to unfold. Then I jumped in my Humvee and told my driver to go as fast as he could—directly toward the smoke.

CHAPTER 3

Commanding Courage

In the military, they teach you to move toward the sound of gunfire. That's what we were doing. It's the same impulse firefighters have to rush into a burning building. It takes courage, and I don't say that in a boastful way at all. I say that because I know where my source of courage comes from.

My courage comes from God.

When my driver, Pete Bazcek, and I reached the motor pool, we found that a vehicle had caught fire and was about to explode. I ordered the evacuation of the area and jumped into the vehicle to try to put the fire out. The back of the vehicle was filled with ammunition. If that fire kept burning, we were going to have a disaster of epic proportions on our hands.

The evacuation was nearly completed when I finally had no choice but to give up my fight against the flames and run from the vehicle as fast as I could. The fire was just too hot, and it was spreading too quickly. I'd barely managed to hit the dirt behind another truck for protection when the vehicle exploded, detonating thousands of pounds of ammunition along with it.

The concussion of the explosion set off other explosions, which lit other fires, sending flames and smoke billowing like some tower from Hell into the sky above. But I was not afraid. Even though my ears were ringing and the whole world seemed muffled around me, even though I could barely breathe in the blackness of that smoke, I stood up and spent the next six hours in the middle of that motor pool with my driver, helping people who hadn't made it out in time, pulling some of them out from under trucks where they'd hid and were trapped. There was unexploded ordinance all around, and the fire burned so hot that some tanks and trucks were reduced to nothing but piles of molten metal. But no one died on my watch. Everyone who was in that motor pool made it out alive.

People ask me sometimes, "How were you able to find the courage to do that?"

"It was easy," I say. "I knew God was with us."

Like a Stone Wall

I am not the first military leader to turn to God for strength and courage.

Far from it.

When I was a cadet at West Point, I was awestruck to learn of a particular statement Confederate General Stonewall Jackson made, right in the middle of the Civil War: "My religious beliefs teach me to feel as safe in battle as in bed. God has fixed the time of my death. I do not concern myself with that, but to always be ready whenever it may overtake me. That is the way all men should live, and all men would be equally brave."

As safe in battle as in bed? Just the idea of that was staggering to me. I couldn't understand it—until I lived it.

I was only about five years into my life as a baptized Christian when that motor pool blew up, yet I knew for certain: having walked away from that situation unscathed, having helped to make sure everyone involved got out alive, was by no means my own doing. When I felt God's presence, I felt no fear.

Jackson earned his nickname because even in the heat of battle, he would stand unflinching, immovable, like a "stone wall." How was he able to do that? I believe it's because he was a deacon in his Presbyterian Church back home. It was the fear of God that made him fearless in everything else. He, like Robert E. Lee, always protected his Sundays in order to worship, and he gave all praise, in all things, to God.

Are all of these things unrelated? Did one not have to do with the other? It seems illogical to me to ignore the words of the man himself, when he said it was his "religious beliefs" that gave him his feeling of safety no matter the circumstance.

When I put God first in my life at the age of 32, I aspired to that. I wanted to live my life the Stonewall Jackson way. And so, I prayed. I gave all glory to God. And time and time again, God gave me the courage I needed. This may sound callous, but I don't recall ever being afraid in any of my military endeavors—not when the motor pool blew up, not when I was in Kosovo trying to keep the Serbs from killing the Albanians, not when I was in Athens on a security mission during the Greek Olympics under what may have been the greatest threat of terrorism the Olympic Games had known up until that point in history.

By the time I got to Iraq, I had so much faith that God was protecting me, I was truly able to walk around like Stonewall Jackson in my daily endeavors.

There was more than one occasion where I wound up locked in negotiations with a room full of insurgents, all of them blood-thirsty in their hatred of Americans—yet I did so without a weapon, and without any fear, knowing that God would pull me through. That is just how powerful the courage of God can be.

My battle space during the Surge in 2007 was the size of the state of West Virginia. That was a lot of ground to cover with the 25,000 troops under my command. So we established sixty-two patrol bases, which I visited on a near-daily basis. I spent 624 hours in the back of a Black Hawk helicopter flying fast and low, so we wouldn't get hit by the rockets and machine-gun fire. Flying from point A to B, we were always shot at. The enemy could tell when it was a general officer flying around, because we flew in two helicopters. Sometimes I was in the lead helicopter and sometimes I was in the trail helicopter, just to mix things up.

Because the enemy had heat-seeking missiles in their arsenal, we had flares that would pop out of your helicopter to draw the missiles away. Routinely, I remember sitting in the back of the Black Hawk watching these flares pop out, which let me know that the system had detected some kind of incoming missile that was aimed right at me.

Still, I wasn't scared.

One time I landed at a patrol base, within an established perimeter of sandbags, Bradleys, and barbed-wire, and the moment we touched down we were ambushed. We came under machine-gun fire and mortar attack, and I got right out of that helicopter and started walking toward the base without any hesitation. I wasn't ducking or crawling or anything. I just walked across the sand as if I were walking across a parking lot back home. I had a five-person personal security detachment who traveled with me, and they were frustrated. The non-commissioned officer in charge was a staff sergeant who weighed about 280 pounds and stood 6' 4", and his one job out there was to protect me from harm. So he physically threw me to the ground and laid on me until the attack ended. He couldn't understand why I just kept walking even though there were mortar rounds and machine-gun fire coming in.

I actually chuckled to myself, thinking maybe I'd taken my sense of courage a little too far. I remember lying on the ground and thinking back to Stonewall Jackson: "I'm as relaxed in the bed as I am in battle." It was remarkable to me, but that's exactly how I felt.

I simply wasn't afraid.

I wasn't even afraid *in* my bed in that combat setting, even though at any point on any given night it was entirely possible that a mortar could come flying in and take you out. The enemy, the coward that he is, used indirect fire. He could launch a mortar round and run away, then launch another mortar round and run away, because it took our systems a while to detect the places where the mortar rounds were being launched.

Incoming rounds killed a number of my soldiers and almost killed me on a couple of occasions. One time, I was standing in line going into the fitness center at the Forward Operating Base (FOB) and a mortar round came in and killed the soldier standing just three people ahead of me. And this was supposed to be a relatively secure area.

That attack happened in Baghdad at a major compound we were on one random morning. I mean, in that environment, you were never safe. When people talk about "FOB rats"—people who served in roles that didn't require them to ever leave the FOB, as if they were never at risk—it makes me mad because it's just not true. Of the 153 youngsters who were killed while under my command during the Surge, 15 or 20 of them were killed on a FOB by incoming mortar rounds, and that included a young female sergeant. So you were never safe, not even when you were sleeping.

Sarah described my sleeping accommodations in Iraq as "a dumpster with a door," and that's basically what it looked like. It was a metal container with a door in it, and a bed inside. And every time you climbed into your dumpster to sleep at night, you weren't really sure if you were going to wake up the next day because mortar rounds or rockets could come and take you out.

Still, I slept like a baby. I'm a guy who requires seven hours of sleep every night in order to function, and unless there were extenuating circumstances, I got my seven hours every night in Iraq. That was just a part of my overall physical fitness routine.

How could I do that? Because the most important part of my survival and success over there was, without a doubt, my *spiritual* fitness. I prayed before every mission. I prayed every morning. I prayed every night. I thanked God for protecting my troops. I thanked God for protecting my family back home, and the families of those who so valiantly served their country. I led Bible studies for anyone who wanted to participate, too, continuing the outreach I'd learned through Joe Miller and the Officer's Christian Fellowship way back at Fort Leavenworth. And all of that is what allowed me to bask in the courage of knowing that God was there for me and my family.

The Power of Prayer

Stonewall Jackson wasn't my only inspiration when it came to commanding courage. There are numerous examples going back all through America's military history, through world history, and all the way back (once again) to the Old Testament.

One of the more recent and more prominent figures to put his trust in God on the battlefield was none other than General George S. Patton, the brash World War II hero, whom I'm guessing most people don't think of as a man of faith first. But that's exactly what he was.

Patton was raised in the Episcopal Church and was a regular churchgoer. As a kid, Patton prayed nightly to a picture of two men he thought were God and Jesus. In actuality it was a photo of Robert E. Lee and Stonewall Jackson. I guess that set him up pretty well for a life in the Army.

I find it no coincidence that at one point in the movie *Patton*, someone refers to George Patton as "the greatest general since Stonewall Jackson." They were connected through something much deeper than war. They were connected in their powerful shared faith.

During the Battle of the Bulge, one of the most important battles of World War II, Patton put the power of faith into action—with results that seem downright Biblical in proportion.

It was December of 1944. We had successfully stormed the beach at Normandy and pushed Hitler's Army back across much of France, but the advancement of the Third Army had been stopped in its tracks by three months of nonstop, unforgiving rain. Hitler's Army surged in a massive offensive. We were caught in a crucial battleground in the fight to defeat the evil march of Hitler's Army, and the rains made it impossible for our Army to get a leg up.

On December 8, the Third Army's Chief Chaplain, James H. O'Neill, who was on the ground at Third Army headquarters in France, received a phone call from Patton himself. (O'Neill recounted this story in an official government document in 1950, and the full account of the events that followed is available to anyone who wants to read it. But I'll summarize it for you here, drawing from that document.)

"This is General Patton," he said. "Do you have a good prayer for weather? We must do something about those rains if we are to win the war."

When they got off the phone, Chaplain O'Neill did some reading and couldn't find anything that fit this exact situation the Third Army was in, so instead, he sat down and wrote a prayer that would become known the world over as "Patton's Prayer":

> Almighty and most merciful Father, we humbly beseech Thee, of Thy great goodness, to restrain these immoderate rains with which we have had to contend. Grant us fair weather for Battle. Graciously hearken to us as soldiers who call upon Thee that, armed with Thy power, we may advance from victory to victory, and crush the oppression and wickedness of our enemies and establish Thy justice among men and nations.

Patton was so taken by that prayer, he asked the chaplain to print 250,000 copies of it and distribute it to every soldier under his command. Then he asked Chaplain O'Neill to sit down for a moment. As O'Neill recalls it, Patton "leaned back in his swivel chair, toying with a long lead pencil between his index fingers."

"Chaplain," Patton said, "I am a strong believer in prayer. There are three ways that men get what they want; by planning, by working, and by praying. Any great military operation takes careful planning, or thinking. Then you must have well-trained troops to carry it out: that's working. But between the plan and the operation there is always an unknown. That unknown spells defeat or victory, success or failure. It is the reaction of the actors to the ordeal when it actually comes. Some people call that getting the breaks; I call it God. God has His part, or margin in everything. That's where prayer comes in. Up to now, in the Third Army, God has been very good to us. We have never retreated; we have suffered no defeats, no famine, no epidemics. This is because a lot of people back home are praying for us. We were lucky in Africa, in Sicily, and in Italy. Simply because people prayed. But we have to pray for ourselves too. A good soldier is not made merely by making him think and work. There is something in every soldier that goes deeper than thinking or working—it's his 'guts.' It is something that he has built in there: it is a world of truth and power that is higher than himself. Great living is not all output of thought and work. A man has to have intake as well. I don't know what you call it, but I call it religion, prayer, or God."

Patton went on to make a request: "I wish you would put out a Training Letter on this subject of prayer to all the chaplains; write about nothing else, just the importance of prayer. Let me see it before you send it. We've got to get not only the chaplains but every man in the Third Army to pray. We must ask God to stop these rains. These rains are that margin that hold defeat or victory. If we all pray, it will be like what Dr. Carrel said, it will be like plugging in on a current whose source is in Heaven. I believe that prayer completes that circuit. It is power." The allusion was to a quote Patton had read previously from Dr. Alexis Carrel, one of the foremost scientists at the time, who described prayer "as one of the most powerful forms of energy man can generate."

Chaplain O'Neill did exactly what Patton asked. He printed 250,000 copies of "Patton's Prayer" and distributed it to every soldier in the Third Army. He then wrote a missive on the power of prayer, titled "Training Letter No. 5," and had that distributed not only to all 486 chaplains, but to every organization commander down to and including the regimental level.

Training Letter No. 5 echoed Patton's own words, starting with, "At this stage of the operations I would call upon the chaplains and the men of the Third United States Army to focus their attention on the importance of prayer," and it went on to lay out a very clear objective:

> "Urge all of your men to pray, not alone in church, but everywhere. Pray when driving. Pray when fighting. Pray alone. Pray with others. Pray by night and pray by day. Pray for the cessation of immoderate rains, for good weather for Battle. Pray for the defeat of our wicked enemy whose banner is injustice and whose good is oppression. Pray for victory. Pray for our Army, and Pray for Peace.
>
> "We must march together, all out for God. The soldier who 'cracks up' does not need sympathy or comfort as much as he needs strength. We are not trying to make the best of these days. It is our job to make the most of them. Now is not the time to follow God from 'afar off.' This Army needs the assurance and the faith that God is with us. With prayer, we cannot fail."

As you may have concluded by now, I believe that message is as useful in daily life as it is in war.

The results of putting the power of hard work and prayer into action, the way General Patton insisted, were undeniable.

"Patton's Prayer" was distributed across the Third Army between the December 12 and 15, 1944. Training Letter No. 5 went out to all of the leadership right on its heels. And the entire Third Army started praying, all at once.

It had been raining without stopping since September of that year. On December 20, the weather started to ease up. Our Army was finally able to receive air support as the bombers flew in by the hundreds, and then thousands. By December 24, we were able to stall the German advance for the first time since the battle began. Then, on December 26, 1944—the day after Christmas—with the weather cleared, Gen. Patton's 4th Armored Division was able to break through the German front and open a corridor to the besieged town of Bastogne. It was the turning point that won the battle, and set us on a course for pushing the Germans out of France and all the way back to their homeland.

The next time O'Neill saw Patton in person was in Luxembourg, in January of 1945. O'Neill recalled: "He stood directly in front of me, [and] smiled: 'Well, Padre, our prayers worked. I knew they would.' Then he cracked me on the side of my steel helmet with his riding crop. That was his way of saying, 'Well done.'"

Where on Earth did Patton ever get the idea that God would change the weather for the sake of our Army in the heat of war?

There is no doubt that he got the idea from the Bible.

O'Neill wrote that Patton spoke specifically about Gideon when he spoke about the power of prayer, and the story of Gideon is outlined in the Book of Judges. Essentially what happened is this: God came to Gideon and gave him the mission of leading the Israelites against the Midianites, a seemingly insurmountable task given the resources available. Gideon's first response, much like Moses' response to the idea of leading the Israelites out of Egypt, was to highlight his own perceived limitations (Judges 6:15-16):

> "But Lord," Gideon asked, "how can I save Israel? My clan is the weakest in Manasseh, and I am the least in my family." The Lord answered, "I will be with you, and you will strike down all the Midianites together."

God assured Gideon that He would be with him, and He was. Gideon set about the task at hand. He first assembled his forces, a total of 22,000 men. He wasn't convinced that would be enough, but God told Gideon it was too many. He told Gideon to release those Israelites who were too terrified to fight, and 12,000 of them left. With a force of just 10,000, Gideon was worried it wasn't going to be enough to get the job done. But God said it was still too many, so He developed a test, and only 300 of the troops passed the test. Gideon went into battle leading a force of 300 men against a much larger force, and prevailed.

Why? Because God was with him.

As it says in Romans 8:31:

> If God is for us, who can be against us?

In that battle, Gideon, like Patton, like all good leaders, led from the front. "Watch me," he told them. "Follow my lead." (Judges 7:17). And after the victory, Gideon gave all glory to God. Gideon told those he defeated, "I will not rule over you, nor will my son rule over you. The Lord will rule over you." (Judges 8:23).

It's easy to draw the line between Gideon and Patton.

Interestingly enough, I had a similar situation when I deployed the US Army's Third Infantry Division to Iraq as part of the Surge in 2007. I mentioned before that I was given a battle space the size of the state of West Virginia, with only 25,000 troops to cover the area. The thing I didn't mention is that the area was referred to as the "Triangle of Death," due to the large number of insurgents who had been there for years. Not only were we facing a dangerous situation with a relatively small number of soldiers, but we were given next to no time to prepare for the battle. When the surge was announced, we had just begun a training mission that was supposed to last six months, preparing us to go into a more peaceful region in Northern Iraq. I was suddenly ordered to take my 25,000 soldiers to the Triangle of Death in only six-weeks' time.

It seemed impossible. A lot of folks might have whined and complained, or tried to fight the order and change the plan, but all that would have done was wasted what little valuable time we had to prepare. So what I did, just like Moses did, just like Gideon did, was pray. I prayed to God for guidance and courage, and I asked all those under my command to do the same, if they so chose—and I know a whole lot of them followed through, because, just like Patton, I saw the results.

After fifteen months, the area once referred to as the "Triangle of Death" earned a new nickname: "Triangle of Life." (There's a full accounting of what we did to turn that area around in my first book, *Adapt or Die*.) That seemingly miraculous turnaround was all due to the great work of the magnificent Soldiers under my command, but I take no credit for the success. I give all glory to God.

The Walls Came Down

There are eleven passages in the Bible which deal with courage, and perhaps the most famous of them is Joshua 1:9:

> Have I not commanded you? Be strong and courageous. Do not be terrified; do not be discouraged for the Lord your God will be with you wherever you go.

Joshua was Moses's aide. After Moses died, Joshua was empowered by the Lord to pick up the leadership mantle and go on. (Interestingly enough, there's a parallel that could be drawn there to a man I mentioned in the previous chapter, Harry Truman, who had to pick up the mantle of the Presidency in the wake of FDR's death. That parallel had never occurred to me before I started writing this book.)

The Lord told Joshua that no one would ever be able to stand up to him, and that He would never leave Joshua or forsake him. Joshua didn't fully believe it, of course. (There's a pattern here, if you haven't noticed.) He protested, he said he wasn't worthy, he complained that he had all sorts of shortcomings and limitations in life and there was no way he could do the things God wanted him to do. So, just to prove his point, God gave Joshua a series of impossible tasks, including seizing the city of Jericho, which was surrounded by tremendous walls and a gate through which "No one went out, and no one came in." (Joshua 6:1)

Joshua's small army would never have had the strength to break through those walls, were it not for God. With God, all it took was a shout—"the wall collapsed; so everyone charged straight in, and they took the city." (Joshua 6:20)

There's a direct line between Patton and Joshua as well, because just as Patton asked God to change the weather, Joshua once asked for God to halt the movement of the sun and the moon, in order to give his army more time to fight. And guess what? The Lord answered that prayer as well, as described in Joshua 10:12-13:

> On the day the Lord gave the Amorites over to Israel, Joshua said to the Lord in the presence of Israel:
> "Sun, stand still over Gibeon,
> and you, moon, over the Valley of Ajalon."
> So the sun stood still,
> and the moon stopped,
> till the nation avenged itself on[a] its enemies,
> as it is written in the Book of Jashar.
> The sun stopped in the middle of the sky and delayed going down about a full day.

The miracles of God's actions aren't something we can command at will. None of us should ever be boastful or grandiose in thinking that God answers all prayers—even those of great leaders—with whatever a person wants. That would be absurd. God does as God wishes.

I know this can be confusing. It's been confusing to me many times over the years. After all, the Bible also tells us, in Matthew 7:7:

> Ask and it will be given to you; seek and you will find; knock and the door will be opened to you.

I truly believe that God answers all prayers—but sometimes His answer is "No," and sometimes the answer is, "Not right now." And we may not always agree with God's decisions. But that does not mean we shouldn't trust them. Because if we trust in God, we're going to be okay. No matter what. That is what living the Faith of the Centurion is all about: Knowing that no matter how much we think we're in charge of here on Earth, God is always above us, and with us.

I want to repeat Joshua 1:9 here because I think it's one of the most powerful passages in the Bible:

> Have I not commanded you? Be strong and courageous. Do not be terrified; do not be discouraged for the Lord your God will be with you wherever you go.

Knowing that God is with us wherever we go is an amazing source of strength. And that source of strength carries far beyond any battlefield.

Think about all the things we could worry about on any given day. We could worry about natural disasters, like tornadoes and earthquakes. We could worry about the economy. We could worry about domestic terrorism. We could spend every minute of every day worrying about something. It takes courage to get behind the wheel of a car, knowing that any other driver on the road could suddenly veer into your lane and end your life in an instant. It takes courage to get on an airplane, knowing that if those engines should fail, for any reason, there is no way out, and no way to save yourself from crashing.

But living the Faith of the Centurion and trusting that God will come through allows you *not* to worry—about any of these things.

God tells us so, in Matthew 6:25-34:

Therefore I tell you, do not worry about your life, what you will eat or drink; or about your body, what you will wear. Is not life more than food, and the body more than clothes? Look at the birds of the air; they do not sow or reap or store away in barns, and yet your heavenly Father feeds them. Are you not much more valuable than they? Can any one of you by worrying add a single hour to your life?

And why do you worry about clothes? See how the flowers of the field grow. They do not labor or spin. Yet I tell you that not even Solomon in all his splendor was dressed like one of these. If that is how God clothes the grass of the field, which is here today and tomorrow is thrown into the fire, will he not much more clothe you—you of little faith? So do not worry, saying, 'What shall we eat?' or 'What shall we drink?' or 'What shall we wear?' For the pagans run after all these things, and your heavenly Father knows that you need them. But seek first his kingdom and his righteousness, and all these things will be given to you as well. Therefore do not worry about tomorrow, for tomorrow will worry about itself. Each day has enough trouble of its own.

Earlier in this book I had mentioned a similar line from Luke: "*Who of you by worrying can add a single hour to your life?*" Just that one line is powerful, but in this Matthew version—in the context of the entire passage—it truly is stunning. God tells us not to worry about tomorrow, not to worry about our finances, or ability to feed or clothe ourselves. Do not worry about *anything!*

There is only one way I know to accomplish that, and that is through doing my best to live the Faith of the Centurion. By working hard, and praying hard, and giving all glory to God.

The result of living that life shows up all the time. In fact, it showed up dramatically even after I transitioned out of the Army and back into civilian life.

In April of 2012, Sarah and I moved from Central Texas into the Dallas Metroplex when I took on a new job at the University of Texas at Arlington. The very day after we arrived, we received a rude welcome to a part of Texas that's known as Tornado Alley. Sarah was setting up our new on-campus apartment, and I was in a meeting with the University President when the skies turned dark, powerful storms rushed in, and the tornado sirens went off. They hustled everybody down into the basement, and I started to head out the door to get to Sarah and make sure she was safe. "You can't leave!" they said, and someone tried to block my way.

I said, "My wife is by herself in the apartment and there's no way I'm going to stay here." So against all objections, I opened the door and walked across the campus in the middle of this powerful storm to rendezvous with my wife. I wasn't going to let her be by herself in that storm. No way! Everyone else was freaked out and worried about my safety. But I wasn't worried, because God tells me, "Don't worry."

No fewer than twelve tornadoes touched down within a twenty-mile radius of our new home that day. *Twelve.* That's quite the welcome. But I wasn't scared by any of it.

Once again, I don't say that to be boastful. I'm not boasting at all. What I'm saying is that I didn't *have* to be scared because I knew God was with me. In fact, as I've learned over the course of the last thirty years, not being boastful is an important part of this whole journey of faith. It's an incredibly important piece of the puzzle when it comes to living the Faith of the Centurion.

No matter how powerful you think you are, how rich you think you are, how important you think you are, if you want to enjoy God's courage, God's blessings, and God's peace, you have to recognize that God is always above you, and as hard as it is for some people to understand, we all have to learn to be humble.

CHAPTER 4

Being Humble

Remember when I noted there are eleven different passages about courage in the Bible? When something gets repeated that frequently in one book, chances are it's a fairly important message that we ought to be paying attention to.

Well, guess how many passages you'll find in the Bible about humility?

Thirty-three.

Thirty-three!

So, just how important do you think humility is in God's eyes?

Staying humble is an absolute key to living the way God wants us to live, and the proof is found over and over again in Scripture.

Go ahead and pull any of those passages out for a read and you'll quickly discover the message, repeated loud and clear. In fact, let's go ahead and do that right now. Let's sample a few of those verses at random.

How about Philippians 2:3:

> Do nothing out of selfish ambition or vain conceit. Rather, in humility value others above yourselves.

That's certainly a clear message. How about Ephesians 4:2:

> Be completely humble and gentle; be patient, bearing with one another in love.

Be *completely* humble, and gentle. Certainly no ambiguity there. Let's turn to Romans 12:16:

> Live in harmony with one another. Do not be proud, but be willing to associate with people of low position. Do not be conceited.

Oh, that's a good one. I talked about that exact same idea, the importance of leading by walking around, talking to and listening to and caring about your employees or subordinates, as one of my leadership principles in *Adapt or Die*. What the Bible is telling us here is how important it is to have humility not just in your work, but also in life. The same sentiment is echoed and amplified in Colossians 3:12:

> Therefore, as God's chosen people, holy and dearly loved, clothe yourselves with compassion, kindness, humility, gentleness, and patience.

The payoff of that type of leadership is huge. What will the Lord do for you if you are humble before him? The answer lies in James 4:10…

> Humble yourselves before the Lord and He will lift you up.

…and repeated in 1 Peter 5:6:

> Humble yourselves, therefore, under God's mighty hand, that he may lift you up in due time.

The "in due time" part suggests we need to not only be humble, but be patient, too, which is not always easy. But clearly, the whole "patience is a virtue" idea is an important one when it comes to leading a life that leads to achieving inner peace. Being impatient is the thing that often leads us to get upset, filled with anxiety, tending toward road rage and all the sorts of things that can ruin a lot of people's whole day, or week, or month, or year. Those who are humble seem to automatically have more patience for some reason. Think about that.

And then there's the passage that gives me goose bumps—a passage that, I truly believe, holds the key to relieving the anxiety and chaos that seems to be gripping our entire nation. In 2 Chronicles 7:14, God tells us:

> If my people, who are called by my name, will humble themselves and pray and seek my face and turn from their wicked ways, then I will hear from heaven, and I will forgive their sin and will heal their land.

It is an absolutely amazing concept, and it seems like it should be a pretty easy one for us to accomplish: If we would just get our act together and turn to God, turn away from our wicked ways, humble ourselves, and pray, God promises that He will heal our land. When I think about the power of prayer in action, as seen on the battlefield presented in the last chapter—at the Battle of the Bulge—and in the extraordinary accomplishments of my soldiers in Iraq, how can this passage not excite the heck out of me?

The Bible tells us that we have the power to earn God's forgiveness, and that in humbling ourselves, we can earn the attention of God in heaven to come and heal our land. If that's not a reason for every one of us to *want* to be humble, I don't know what is.

Perhaps that's what God is trying to tell us through a modern-day messenger by the name of Tim McGraw too. If you're not familiar with Tim, he's a huge star in the country music world. He's married to another well-known singer by the name of Faith Hill. In early 2016, he released a song entitled "Humble and Kind." It was written by a songwriter named Lori McKenna, and not only did the song become a big hit, rocketing to number-one on the country charts in the U.S. and Canada, but the video for the song and the lyrics to that song went viral. It got so much attention, he even put out a book expanding on its meaning and message. Which means that the song's message—which I believe is a message God wants us to hear—has now been shared by tens of millions of people all over the world.

The song implores listeners to stay humble and kind—not just every once in a while, but *always*. It talks about simple things that could be summed up as a lesson in manners: things like holding the door, and saying please and thank you. It lists some Biblical lessons too, like, you really shouldn't cheat or lie. It also doles out some lessons of the heart. But the part that really gets me comes toward the end of the song, when it says, "When you get where you're goin', don't forget—turn back around and help the next one in line."

Whenever I talk about this song at an event, people perk up, even if they're not country music fans. I'm not sure what it is about the way the words and music come together just right, but somehow, it seems like everyone can relate—especially to the idea that when you get to the front of the line, you ought to turn around, look back and help the next person. I *love* that phrase! I've found so much satisfaction and joy in my life by giving back, by being a mentor, by helping other people to climb up the ladder behind me along the way.

There's power in that—real power that pays off in unimaginably positive ways.

The biggest, of course, being the inner peace that comes with living the way God wants us to live.

Personal Humility

So we've got the Bible telling us to be humble going all the way back to ancient times, and we've got Tim McGraw telling us to be humble in 2016. Seems like something we ought to be paying attention to.

I somehow managed to get an early start on the road to humility, long before I was baptized. For instance, I never walked around wearing my West Point ring. Some people wear that ring as a badge of honor, and it most certainly is an honor to have graduated from that elite academy. I just never wanted to be the guy who paraded around the Army saying, "Look at me. I'm a West Pointer. I'm somebody special so you should give me some special dispensation or compensation." I guess I had a natural desire for humility from the start.

I really started paying attention to staying humble after I was baptized, though. I mean, I was pretty proud of myself for getting promoted to the rank of major just before my baptism, but with every single promotion that followed, I gave all glory to God. In fact, for the last thirty years, I've given all glory to God and all thanks to my family for every great thing that has come my way. I'm humble enough to realize that a lot of things I obtain are not because of my own capabilities or my own merits, but instead are by the grace of God.

Living with that kind of humility is exactly what God wants us to do.

I'll share with you something here I don't talk about a lot—something I feel less than humble even mentioning in my books and speeches, yet something that feels necessary to help make this point about humility. Two other soldiers and I were awarded the Soldier's Medal in Doha, Kuwait, for risking our lives to save others when the motor pool blew up. For those who don't know, the Soldier's Medal is the highest award you can receive in peacetime for heroism. It's like the peacetime version of the Medal of Honor. To get one of those medals, you have to risk your life to save others.

Out of a sense of humility, I never made that medal a badge of honor. I didn't order a special commemorative license plate. In fact, when people find out I have a Soldier's Medal, they're sometimes surprised that it's never come up in conversation. Even though General Norman Schwarzkopf himself flew in to personally pin those medals on our uniforms, I just never wanted to make it a big deal.

Why?

Because I knew our courage and good fortune that day were all God's doing, not my own. I am simply humbled and thankful that neither my life nor any of my soldiers' lives were lost.

It wasn't long after that incident in Kuwait when I was selected to become a Brigadier General. The United States has a million-man army, and on any given day there's only three-hundred or so general officers, so it's a pretty steep cut. I was in Washington, D.C. when I got that call, and Sarah was back in Texas. We had been separated by the requirements of my job for many months, which was hard, and which tore at me—but when I got that call telling me I was being promoted to Brigadier General, my eyes filled with tears and I thanked God for the opportunity to serve the nation in such an important way. I realized the sacrifices I was making in working so hard for the Army—and the sacrifices my family was making in order to support my career—must've aligned with what God wanted.

The sacrifices were worth it.

The key to staying humble, though, was to remember how unimportant I really was in the grand scheme of things. When getting promoted to general officer, or to senior vice president, or CEO, or even getting elected to Congress or the White House—it's pretty easy to convince yourself you're a little bit better than everyone else. But thankfully, as I developed a routine of Bible study every morning, I was constantly reminded by those thirty-three citations of Scripture just how important humility was in God's eyes.

I had other reminders too.

Back when I was selected for battalion command, the division commander told me, "The last promotion and position you attain based on your own merit is Lieutenant Colonel and Battalion Command. Everything after that will be based on the needs of the Army at the particular time."

That was his way of telling me not to get a big head if I got promoted further, and not to feel bad if I didn't get promoted, either. After all, it's a rare thing for *anyone* to move beyond the rank of Lieutenant Colonel in the Army. But for whatever reason, I continued to get promoted on an accelerated timeline, which we in the Army refer to as getting promoted below the zone. And I felt humbled at every step.

Once I was a general officer, I took it upon myself to remind others that they ought to feel humbled, too. Every time there was a General Officer Selection Board and the results were announced, I wrote a personal letter to the selectees and reminded them that they were nobody special.

"People are going to treat you different," I told them.

That's true of anyone in a high position. As soon as you become a general officer, people think you're somebody important. They want to treat you different even though you're still the same person you were before you put on the star. So I reminded every new general officer from the time I got selected for promotion to the time I retired, via personal letter, "Don't get a big head. Just because you got selected doesn't mean that you're better than everybody else."

As a leader and a servant of Christ, you have to remind yourself of that. When everybody's scurrying around trying to make you happy in the hopes of getting into your good graces, you have to routinely try to do more yourself, and do more for them, rather than allowing people to do things for you. If you're in a high position, don't believe the hype. Don't believe your own press. Stay grounded. Stay humble and kind. That's the way God wants it. And there is peace in that.

One of my mentors, General Scott Wallace, who was one of my commanders in the 11th Armored Cavalry Regiment in Fulda, Germany, put it another way. When I was selected, he said, "Look, just remember, you're not better looking than you used to be and your jokes aren't any funnier than they used to be, but people *will* treat you different."

His words were so true. When I got that first star, next thing I knew I had people surrounding me who never would have come up to me before, and they were laughing at things I said even though whatever I said wasn't particularly funny!

I just kept telling myself, "Stay humble, Rick. Stay humble and the Lord will lift you up."

Staying Humble in Higher Office

The idea of humility bears itself out not only in the Bible, but also in American history. There are plenty of people who've risen to far higher positions than I have while remaining humble throughout their careers, including two influential Presidents from two very different eras.

The first that comes to my mind is a fellow Texan: George H.W. Bush. Sarah and I have had the pleasure of meeting President Bush and his wife, Barbara, at St. Martin's Episcopal Church here in the Lone Star State, and they're both lovely people.

No matter what you may think about his politics (or his son's politics), I don't think anyone can deny that our

President Bush is a humble guy. Of all the Presidents we've had in the last few decades, can you think of another that showed his level of humility? I sure can't.

George H.W. Bush enlisted in the U.S. Navy at the age of 18. His plane was hit by enemy fire on September 2, 1944, and he was awarded a Distinguished Flying Cross and three Air Medals. He certainly had a lot to brag about at a young age. But when it came to humility, Bush learned a valuable lesson from his mother.

"George," she told him, "never brag."

Never brag. That's a nice clear, concise rule. I like that rule!

As an Episcopalian, Bush seemed to always work hard to lead a good Christian life. "I am guided by certain traditions," he wrote. "One is that there is a God and He is good, and His love while free has a self-imposed cost: We must be good to one another."

How great would it be if all Presidents taught that lesson from the pulpit of the White House? I'd be happy to get in line behind any President who exuded those values.

The second President that comes to mind is Ulysses S. Grant—the other leading Civil War General whose portrait loomed so prominently over all of us cadets at West Point.

Grant wasn't a man who went to church. (He said he didn't like the music.) Yet he, like Bush, looked to the teachings of his mother as a guide in life—and that guide served him well. As a youngster, Grant's mother taught him not to talk back to people who teased him. She taught him to always keep his dignity in that way, which is a part of staying humble, honorable, and focused in life. Shouting, arguing back, or escalating personal conflict in order to deflect or relieve an attack on one's ego is the exact opposite of being humble; it's the exact opposite of turning the other cheek, which even the non-Christians among us seem to recognize as a common, familiar phrase from the Bible. The actual quote is Matthew 5:38-39:

> "You have heard that it was said, 'Eye for eye, and tooth for tooth.' But I tell you, do not resist an evil person. If anyone slaps you on the right cheek, turn to them the other cheek also.

That whole passage of the Bible, which goes on to say, "Love thy enemy," is sometimes difficult to understand in the context of war. The fact is, there are enemies; there are forces that rise up with the aim of defeating the best of humanity and destroying the good work that has been done in God's name. Those enemies must be shut down. That's just part of the hard work we're tasked with as children of God. But it doesn't mean you can't love that enemy just the same, and show a sense of humility, even in times of war.

God loves all people. *All* people. And our goal is to try to live like Him.

Grant exemplified this.

He earned praise for his humility from no less a figure than President Abraham Lincoln. Grant was known for carrying out his duties with unquestioned integrity, while never challenging the dignity of others. What a great thing to be known for! And he truly showed, in his actions, that he loved his enemy as God tells us. In his surrender terms at the end of the Civil War,

Grant made it clear that he did not want to humiliate the surrendered Confederate forces; he allowed them to retain their horses and sidearms; and when he learned that Confederate soldiers were starving, Grant sent them rations.

He did what God asks us to do in Matthew 7:12:

> So in everything, do to others what you would have them do to you, for this sums up the Law and the Prophets.

If you want to get really inspired by Grant's humility, pick up a copy of his memoirs. His writings reflect great modesty and restraint, exhibiting candor and a good sense of humor that should serve as an example to all of us.

Grant's life also provides an example of how God elevates and rewards the humble. The fact is, Grant never actually sought higher office. He didn't want it. He was content right where he was, wherever that place might be. Yet he became one of the greatest general officers in history, and went on to be elected President of the United States—at age 44.

That's not bad for a guy who some might judge for not going to church, which reminds me of another part of being humble: *It's not up to us to judge.* As it says in Matthew 7:16-17:

> Do not judge, or you too will be judged. For in the same way you judge others, you will be judged, and with the measure you use, it will be measured to you.

The fact is, Ulysses S. Grant was a baptized Christian who was re-baptized on his deathbed. He was a modern-day Centurion, and I have no doubt whatsoever that he's serving in a high position in heaven.

Living Like a Centurion

The importance of humility is the focus of the one piece of Scripture that exudes the expression of the greatest faith of all—the biblical passage I mentioned so prominently in the introduction to this book—known as the Faith of the Centurion.

In fact, this whole chapter is really about what the Roman Centurion did. Go back and read the passage from the introduction again, or pull out your Bible and read it there. (Matthew 8:5-13).

What the Centurion recognized was that although he was a man of authority with people under him, he could not do this alone. He humbled himself before the Lord Jesus Christ because he knew Jesus could heal his servant, and the Centurion could not. At the end of the day, the Centurion knew he simply wasn't as good and powerful as the Lord. He humbled himself. And in so doing, Jesus recognized that the Centurion had the greatest faith of all.

We all need to pay attention to that. It's okay to admit you're not all things. Only God is all things. You cannot do everything. It is simply impossible. It is okay to humble yourself and ask for help. In fact, it's better than okay. Humbling oneself and asking God for assistance is the way to show God you're a true believer!

With such great faith, all things are possible. *All* things. And I am convinced that anyone who exemplifies the great qualities of that Centurion can elevate him or herself to new heights, new positions, new responsibilities, new growth, new achievements, and a greater fulfillment in life. It's all there for the taking.

Another one of my favorite passages in the Bible, which I referenced strongly in my first book, is known as the Prayer of Jabez. It's found in 1 Chronicles 4:10:

> Jabez cried out to the God of Israel, "Oh, that you would bless me and enlarge my territory! Let your hand be with me, and keep me from harm so that I will be free from pain." And God granted his request.

With humility, with hard work, with prayer, God blesses us—exactly as God blessed Jabez. Remember earlier (back in Chapter 2) when I mentioned God kept giving me more and more blessings, which caused me to have more and more work, which caused me to have more and more responsibilities? I didn't fully understand it at the time, but that was God's work in action. The humbler I became, the more prayer and thankfulness I offered; the more I did my best to live a life in God's image, the more God kept "enlarging my territory." He put me in charge of massive tasks, the likes of which I could only dream of when I was a young cadet. Leading 25,000 troops in Iraq, running Fort Hood, working at the Pentagon, being placed in charge of all Army Installations worldwide, overseeing a workforce of 120,000 military and civilian employees combined—those tasks were actually far bigger than anything I could have dreamed of as a cadet. Yet, He saw me through those challenging tasks. He blessed me with great victories on the battlefield, with powerful decision-making abilities in difficult times, with tremendous courage when courage was needed—all while expanding my family in due time as well. I'm a proud grandfather now, watching my kids as they start their own journeys, raising kids of their own.

And for *all* of that, I am so thankful. I feel *so* blessed.

I am humbled.

From Battlefields to the Gridiron

I've talked about Generals and Presidents in this chapter, but there are all sorts of great leaders out there who've lived humble lives. Keep your eyes open for them. Look to them for inspiration. They're all over the place. And chances are, those who've chosen to live life as Centurions have accomplished some pretty incredible things. Look to the business world. Look to the music world. Look to the sports world. Wherever you find inspiration, you'll find the equivalent of modern-day Centurions. Of course, you'll find plenty of people bragging and showing off and, in some cases, making complete fools of themselves. But quietly, right next to those people—and usually far surpassing them in achievement—are the humble and kind high-achievers who give all glory to God.

One such individual from the world of sports inspired me with his message of humility and strong faith: Tom Landry, the legendary Dallas Cowboys' football coach who, during the course of his twenty-nine years with the Cowboys, led his team to twenty consecutive winning seasons—making him easily one of the greatest football coaches in NFL history.

Years ago, I invited him to speak at a prayer luncheon at Fort Hood, and of course a whole bunch of soldiers turned out to see him. He's a full-blown Texas hero! But while a lot of people turned up expecting to hear from Tom Landry the coach, what they heard was a speech from Tom Landry the Christian.

Landry was yet another reminder of the crucial truth that it's never too late to find faith. He, just like me, like the Apostle Paul and so many others, didn't really start paying attention to God until he was in his early thirties. A friend happened to take him along to a Bible study, and from that moment forward, Landry's life was changed.

He started studying the Bible, and trying live life the way God wants us to live—as a humble man, giving all glory for his team's victories to God—and he attributed his remarkable, lifelong success to that change.

He gave such an inspiring speech that day. I'll never forget it, and I'd venture to say nobody in that room will forget it. The two big takeaways for me were, first, he highlighted the fact that "becoming a Christian was easy, but *being* a Christian is *hard*." He somehow made that message sink in for me more succinctly and poignantly than anyone had up until that point—even though the basic thought behind that message had been bouncing around in my head and my heart since my days at Fort Leavenworth.

He is also the person who so succinctly told the audience, "Being a Christian is not about who you are; it is about what you do." What a message! It hit me as if I was helmeted up in the locker room, about to charge out onto the field after half-time with my sights set on winning the Super Bowl. He so concisely put into one memorable phrase the basic message that so many others had been trying to teach me since I started my Christian Walk. He pointed directly to Scripture to back up his words, too, quoting something I shared with you once already, in the introduction of this book, James 2:17:

> Faith by itself, if it is not accompanied by action, is dead.

What strikes me most about this line of Scripture, and about Tom Landry's missive, is the result of what happens when faith *is* accompanied by action. From the Bible itself, from examples of my own life's lessons, from history, and from influential Christians like Tom Landry, the thing we can all take away from this discussion is this: Faith *in* action is *alive*! Faith *in* action is *powerful*!

Which gets me thinking once more about 2 Chronicles 7:14, where God tells us, "*If my people, who are called by my name, will humble themselves and pray and seek My face and turn from their wicked ways, then I will hear from heaven and forgive their sin and will heal their land.*"

Can we live that way as a nation? Can we come together to pray and lift ourselves up, just as we've been told to do, so that God will come and heal our land?

I'm hopeful. I truly am. I know that with God, all things are possible, and that makes me one heck of an optimist.

Of course, getting the result we're after takes more than simply seeking God, more than just prayer, and more than just being humble. According to that all-important piece of Scripture, the other aspect that's required in order for God to hear us, and heal us, involves turning from our "evil ways"— and that, my friend, is one heck of a challenge.

CHAPTER 5

Growing Beyond
One's Sinful Nature

Searching for answers on the road to finding true inner peace will lead you to some pretty amazing discoveries. For instance, did you know that every one of us is a sinner?

The Bible tells us as much, with no ambiguity, in Romans 3:23:

> ...for all have sinned and fall short of the glory of God...

In some ways, that's a very freeing statement. We've *all* sinned. We *all* fall short of the glory of God. That puts us all on equal footing. I've sinned. You've sinned. The self-righteous guy at work who thinks he's better than everyone else? He's for sure sinned. Your neighbor's sinned. Your President has sinned. Your teacher has sinned. Your parents have sinned. Your preacher has sinned. The Pope has sinned! All of us have sinned and fall short of the glory of God—and chances are every one of us isn't just a sinner in the past tense, but continues to sin and fall short of the glory of God on a fairly regular basis.

That is surely the case with me. I'm not going to sit here and list all of my sins for you, because that isn't helpful to anyone. Frankly, that's between me and God. But I will tell you that I've certainly sinned in the past, and even though I do everything I can to try to avoid sinning now, I still recognize that I'm a sinner in the present.

We "all fall short." That's just a fact. Which begs an important question: If it's an unavoidable fact—if sinning is part of the human condition—then what are we supposed to do about it? How are we supposed to "turn from our evil ways" as God commands?

The answer I've come to after thirty-some years is this: All we can do is *try*. We have to try, and try hard.

What I tell myself all the time is, *Try your best.* Do everything you can to live a good life. You have choices to make in life all the time, and doing your best to choose the right thing, the thing that isn't a sin in any given moment, will leave you feeling better and more at peace when all is said and done. After all, you won't have to feel guilty and anxious if you don't do things that cause you to feel guilty and anxious in the first place.

It all sounds pretty simple, but for some reason, it isn't. It's not that easy to accomplish, or I think we'd all do it. It sure would make life a lot less complicated if we could just stop sinning.

But the Bible seems to be telling us we can't do that. And I think history shows that we can't do that. There is no such perfect person who has ever walked the face of the Earth. So, rather than try to stop sinning altogether, which is apparently an impossible task, one way to try to "turn from evil" is fairly easy: Spend less time doing bad things. The easiest way I've found to do that is to spend *more* time doing *good*.

They say idle hands are the devil's playthings, and there is definitely some truth in that statement. It's easy to find bad things to do when you sit around restless and bored. But I've found that if I fill my time with good things and give my energy toward doing good in the world, if I try my best to spend all of my time living the Faith of the Centurion, there's a whole lot *less* time for sinful activities. That's been especially important to me since I transitioned from the military out into civilian life.

As Sarah and I transitioned from the U.S. Army to our life outside the military, we prayed to God for guidance as to how we should live the rest of our lives. (I never use the word retire. We didn't retire; we just transitioned from one form of service to another.)

As a result of our prayer, God led us to the idea of only doing meaningful and substantive work around people with shared values. We try to follow that idea in everything we do.

One of the things we have a passion for is to help our Nation's military and their families. With budget cuts and sequestration, many of the programs designed to help are being cut or eliminated. We were asked by HEB, a grocery store chain in Texas (and the twelfth-largest privately owned company in the nation) to help design a program which would support the military and their families in the State of Texas. We helped them launch Operation Appreciation, designed to show these folks how much HEB appreciates their service and their sacrifices. Under Operation Appreciation, they build homes for wounded soldiers by partnering with non-profits such as Homes for Our Troops and Operation Finally Home. They help military children through the support of the Military Child Education Coalition (MCEC). They help the survivors of our fallen heroes through their support of Tragedy Assistance Program for Survivors (TAPS). And they support the USO in their efforts to help active duty military transition to civilian life too.

We were also asked by Gary Sinise to serve as Ambassadors and Advisory Board members for the Gary Sinise Foundation. Most folks know Gary as a great actor. We know him as a wonderful humanitarian. Gary truly cares about his fellow human beings. He invests his time, talent, and personal resources every day to help in any way he can. He started the Gary Sinise Foundation to help our nation's first responders and their families, and we are proud to assist him in that important effort. The Gary Sinise Foundation builds homes for severely disabled service members (quadruple and triple amputees), as well as provides entertainment for our troops with Lieutenant Dan Band concerts and Invincible Spirit Events. They honor our World War II Veterans with trips to the World War II museum in New Orleans, and work to support military children through their efforts with Snowball Express, and much, much more.

I can't even count the number of hours I pour into those two nonprofit organizations alone, and that just accounts for part of how we spend our time doing good.

Some people have asked me, though, "Why should we bother doing these sorts of things if we all fall short of God's glory anyway? What's the incentive?"

I can see why people ask those sorts of questions, especially when we see so many "sinners" seemingly getting ahead in life: the greedy bankers, the dishonest politicians, and more. Well, ask yourself what it is you seek. Do you want the torment that comes with being greedy and dishonest? Or do you want the "inner peace" that I went searching for in my early thirties? Do you want to lead a life built on fear and anxiety? Or do you want to live a life free from worry and doubt? Do you want to live a life full of earthly riches, knowing that you can't take it with you? Or do you want to live a life full of all of God's glories and blessings, which will not only enrich you here and now but also for all eternity?

I don't think you'd have bothered to read this far if you didn't truly want the latter in every one of those "what-if" questions. And the fact is, this step of growing beyond our naturally sinful nature is an incredibly important part of the hard work it takes to get to the goal you're after.

Casting Off Sin

In the previous chapter, I mentioned what God wants us to do according to Colossians 3:12: *"clothe yourselves with compassion, kindness, humility, gentleness, and patience."*

What I failed to mention is that in order to accomplish this, you have to cast off a whole lot of sin—which is laid out, in detail, in the words that precede that passage. These are known as the Rules for Holy Living, and here they are in context, Colossians 3:5-12:

> Put to death, therefore, whatever belongs to your earthly nature: sexual immorality, impurity, lust, evil desires, and greed, which is idolatry. Because of these, the wrath of God is coming. You used to walk in these ways, in the life you once lived. But now you must also rid yourselves of all such things as these: anger, rage, malice, slander, and filthy language from your lips. Do not lie to each other, since you have taken off your old self with its practices and have put on the new self, which is being renewed in knowledge in the image of its Creator. Here there is no Gentile or Jew, circumcised or uncircumcised, barbarian, Scythian, slave or free, but Christ is all, and is in all.
>
> Therefore, as God's chosen people, holy and dearly loved, clothe yourselves with compassion, kindness, humility, gentleness, and patience.

That's a lot to let go of, isn't it? I mean, *lust*? Even a faithful, married man is gonna feel attraction, appreciation, and desire sometimes—hopefully he feels it only for his wife, but still. For most men, lust is almost as natural an impulse as breathing. *Anger and rage*? We live in a culture where anger and rage are served up for breakfast on every morning news program. It's hard not to jump into the fray. *Filthy language*? I'm an Army General! People talk about "swearing like a sailor," but I'd put my Army boys up against a bunch of sailors in a swearing competition any day of the week. I used to swear up a storm when I barked orders at my soldiers, and I still catch myself using filthy language now and then. It's something I was raised around in working-class Ohio, and something that certainly seemed par for the course in the Army. It's a habit that's hard to shake, especially when you're out among friends, sharing a glass or two of whiskey.

When it comes to sinning, it often seems to be part of human nature; as if we can't stop ourselves. Even when we want to.

Well, guess what? That's acknowledged in the Bible, too. In Romans 7:15, the Apostle Paul said:

> I do not understand what I do. For what I want to do I do not do, but what I hate I do.

You might have to read that more than once to make sense of it, I realize. But it's worth it. What Paul is saying is that he can't understand why he winds up doing the things he doesn't want to do. It's almost as if it's out of his control. I told you before, I like this Paul guy. He articulates what it means to be human, and I take solace in his words, which reinforce the notion that we *all* fall short.

The Bible tells us pretty clearly that we ought not to fault ourselves for being sinful. But what we *should* do is everything in our power to turn away from those wicked ways—because when we do, God will forgive our sins.

The fact is, there are plenty of well-known individuals who've done extraordinary things, who've lived a life in God's image in astonishing ways, who were also well-known sinners. Two who come to mind for me, having spent some of my formative years in the 1960s, were Martin Luther King Jr. and President John F. Kennedy.

I'm not real comfortable talking about other people's sins, even famous people's sins. Just as I don't want to drag my list of sins into a book for public consumption, it feels wrong to me to drag anyone else's sins into this discussion, either. So I hope I'm forgiven for dredging up old news. I just think it's important to make this point about how we all fall short of the glory of God.

It's been documented that John F. Kennedy had at least seven extramarital affairs, the most famous being with Marilyn Monroe in 1962. It's not uncommon to see Kennedy described as a "compulsive womanizer." We can read about a host of excuses for his behavior, too, ranging from his brush with death in WWII, to his father's conspicuous adultery, to his difficult relationship with his mother. But who are we to judge, right? Kennedy was our nation's only Roman Catholic President. He considered himself a strong Catholic, and I take him at his word on that. I also recognize that he didn't push his religious views on others, calling them his "own private affair."

Given the passion he brought to the Presidency, the number of young people he inspired to get involved in what was going on in Washington, and the way his administration walked us back from the brink of nuclear disaster during the Cuban Missile Crisis, it's easy to see why Kennedy is held in such high regard by so many people—but it's also difficult to recognize where he might stand in God's eyes, given what we know about his personal life.

The same goes for Martin Luther King Jr.

King was an American Baptist minister who had a well-known "weakness for women." His many affairs were well documented, and because of that he was labeled a "hypocritical preacher." He apparently had painful and overwhelming guilt from his affairs, too, but couldn't stop himself; he said they were a "form of anxiety reduction." His wife Coretta even knew of his affairs, yet she has said "all that other business just doesn't have a place in the very high relationship we enjoyed."

How can these two great leaders be considered strong Christians when they went on sinning throughout the entirety of their tragically cut-short lives?

I once again want to point out that it's not up to us to judge. That's God's job. And yet, what we can do is try to learn some lesson from the work these two men did. The fact is, whether or not you believe in their political leanings or ideologies, both of these men had accomplishments in life that far outweighed their sins. Granted, their sins were serious: "Thou shalt not commit adultery" is right there in the Ten Commandments, and I personally have no tolerance for those who would commit adultery. As sins go, that's a big one. But as we look at these men in a historical context, their sins are a relatively minor footnote in the extraordinary lives they led.

And that is where the lesson is found.

Part of living the Faith of the Centurion is the act of *trying* to grow beyond our sinful nature—trying to do fewer bad things on any given day, and striving to do more good things instead.

If I look back on my life, the number of bad things I did in the past clearly outweigh the number of bad things I'm doing right now. And the good things I did in the past are clearly outweighed by the number of good things I'm doing now. It's like a pendulum. As you're attempting to live the life of the Centurion, you're trying to get that pendulum to swing more to the side of doing good and less to the side of doing bad.

I picture it in my mind like a seesaw, or maybe the lady holding the scales of justice—it's my job to try to make the good side rise higher than the bad side, as much as possible, every minute, every hour, every day, for the rest of my life.

For years I've tried to make sense of exactly how God judges these things. For instance, I do not believe if you commit a murder you can simply ask for God's forgiveness, say that you've turned from your "evil ways," and be forgiven and brought into heaven. It can't be that easy. That makes no sense to me, no matter how hard I try to make sense of it. There are degrees of sin in the world. Clearly. My swearing now and then is not the same as committing adultery or committing a murder. I've also had to wrestle profoundly with the idea that the Bible clearly states it is immoral to kill, yet the Bible also shows many great Christians killing in the name of Christ. Not to mention my role in the Army was such that I was responsible for the deaths of many of our enemies and, as is always the case in the course of any war, there were certainly innocent civilians who were killed at times, too.

How can anyone be expected to make sense of all of this, or be at peace with all of this?

The thing I've come to learn is that we humans aren't fully capable of understanding everything God is thinking. We instead have to trust that He knows what He's doing. Finding peace with that is a big part of what faith is all about. I'll get into a deeper discussion of this challenge in Chapter 7.

In the meantime, for many years, I found myself asking time and time again, how can we go on trying to live in God's image when we are constantly tempted and drawn toward sin?

In 1 Corinthians 10:13, we're told:

> No temptation has overtaken you except what is common to mankind. And God is faithful; he will not let you be tempted beyond what you can bear. But when you are tempted, he will also provide a way out so that you can endure it.

There is solace in this passage, once again, as it reinforces the notion that whatever temptation we face (or even succumb to) isn't unique to us. Whatever we go through, it's because all of us are sinners, and all of us fall short of the glory of God. The fact that that particular notion is repeated more than once in the Bible is probably worth paying attention to.

There is also some solace in knowing that God is faithful, of course, and that He won't give us more than we can bear.

But what is this business about giving us a "way out so that you can endure it"?

I'd like to take a few moments to delve into that.

The Punishment of David

The first part of 1 Corinthians 10:13, testifying that any temptation we face has already been faced by men before us, is exemplified in the story of David.

David became the second king of Israel at the age of 30. He was an ancestor of Jesus, and was called "a man after God's own heart." He was a valorous warrior who showed great skills in fighting the Philistines. He was a man of great courage: this is the very same David who defeated the giant Goliath with nothing but a sling and a stone. He was also a poet and musician—an exemplary, well-rounded human being if ever there was one.

Yet, David was a man of many weaknesses. He had many wives, and had an infamous adulterous affair with a married woman—Bathsheba—whom he wanted from the moment he first laid eyes on her, seeing her bathing on her rooftop. He invited her over. He slept with her. He got her pregnant. Then he sent her husband Uriah off to the front lines of combat with the expressed purpose of getting him killed.

This is all detailed in 2 Samuel 11-14. It is quite the story!

The thing that's most striking about David is, as his life went along, he didn't turn from his evil ways. It seems rather, he ran *toward* them. So what are we supposed to take away from that?

It's a pretty straightforward lesson, I think: Don't do what David did!

As a result of his sins, David went from being "a man after God's own heart" to being severely punished by God for his indiscretions. God punished him by killing his son, and then by threatening to send his own wives off to commit adultery with his best friends.

So I guess there are two lessons. One, it's an affirmation that any sin we're tempted by has been a temptation to men before us, because just about every sin you can think of was committed by David alone. But two, it shows that God will actively punish those who continue to sin without remorse, without turning away from their evil ways. I don't know about you, but the idea of being punished by God certainly does not bring me a sense of "inner peace." There's enough struggle in life without purposefully wanting to bring more anguish upon myself. I would much rather do my best to avoid that fate.

So what could David have done, other than not commit those sins in the first place, to get back into God's good graces? What is this "way out" that God provides, as described in 1 Corinthians 10:13?

As I said at the beginning of this chapter, the answer I've found after thirty-plus years of searching for answers is that in order to grow beyond our sinful nature, in order to turn from our evil ways in the eyes of God, we need to at least *try*. We need to make an effort. And one of the best ways to do that is to use a remarkable tool God gives to us freely, to use whenever we desire. A tool called prayer.

A.C.T.S.

I know some people struggle with exactly what a prayer ought to be. Is it a listing off of things we want or need? Is it a confession? What?

As I came to learn in time, it is both—and it is more.

Jesus taught us to pray by using the Lord's Prayer, and following that prayer's structure is a good start. What I do when I'm praying myself is to follow an acronym I learned at church: A.C.T.S. That's short for Acknowledgement, Confession, Thanksgiving, and Supplication. The first thing you do is start with Acknowledgement that God is great. God is good. God is the one who can make all things possible. So you acknowledge His presence. You acknowledge His greatness. C is Confession; right in your prayer, at the beginning, you say, "Man, I screwed up again. All the things I wasn't supposed to do I did, just like the Apostle Paul said." The T is Thanksgiving, where you give God the thanks for all the blessings He's sent your way. And the S is Supplication, those things you want God to do for you. That's where it's okay to say things like Jabez said: "*Oh, that you would bless me and enlarge my territory!*"

So as I do my daily prayers, every single morning before I start my day, I always use that basic structure: acknowledge God's greatness, confess my sins, be thankful for what God has given me, and then ask Him for things. And there's always something for me to talk about when I confess my sins. We all have that. It's nothing to be ashamed of. And by the way, God knows what you are and what you do in the dark. You can't hide it from Him. He already knows what you're doing. So why hide it? He just wants you to acknowledge that what you did was wrong.

We all sin and fall short of the glory of God. And acknowledging those sins, through prayer, is what God wants us to do. As is stated in 1 John 1:8-10:

> If we claim to be without sin, we deceive ourselves and the truth is not in us. If we confess our sins, he is faithful and just and will forgive us our sins and purify us from all unrighteousness. If we claim we have not sinned, we make him out to be a liar and his word is not in us.

I certainly don't want to make God out to be a liar. And I also don't want to deceive myself. So, I confess my sins through prayer daily.

I don't expect anyone to take my directive on any of this, of course. The Bible lays it out pretty clearly, but even that isn't enough incentive for some people to want to actively live a better life. Sometimes, we need to look to other examples to help teach us what to do, and show us how to live like the Centurion.

I don't know about you, but for me, at times, I've mistakenly thought I had things all figured out. I insisted that I could handle everything on my own. Maybe that's just part of the bullheadedness of being young. But even when we grow up and get smart enough to learn that we *don't* know everything, it's easy—especially for those who are fortunate to be placed in positions of leadership—to try to forge forward on our own, and to try to figure everything out by ourselves.

I think there's great danger in that.

If we live like kings, like David did, thinking we're above it all, not bowing down like the Centurion did, not living the way God wants us to live, we will suffer.

That's one reason I've always tried to look toward mentors, not only in my career, but also in my Christian Walk. I want to learn from the example of others whom I admire how to turn away from sin and live a life that's closer to the one God wants us to live.

Maybe if David had had a mentor, he wouldn't have strayed so far.

A Mentor in Good Living

I was fortunate enough to find not just a good mentor, but a great mentor, in General Charles Christopher "Hondo" Campbell.

A renowned and highly decorated Vietnam veteran, Hondo's last assignment before retiring was to take over the leadership of Forces Command, the Army's largest organization, responsible for manning, training, and equipping more than 750,000 soldiers.

General Hondo Campbell was a career mentor for sure, but more important, he was, and still remains, a spiritual mentor of mine. The way he carried himself, the way he spoke, the way he cared for his family—he was always a role model to me. General Campbell was my commanding officer on several occasions during the course of my military career, but more importantly, he was a trusted friend and confidant.

I've noted before that my favorite painting in our home is "The Christian General"—a picture of Robert E. Lee with a small boy and a Bible on his lap. When I close my eyes and picture the modern day Christian General, I see Hondo Campbell.

And even though General Campbell passed away as I was writing this book, I can still feel his presence with me.

General Campbell started every day in prayer. He studied Scripture and was always able to repeat memorized verses. He received his happiness and joy from his personal relationship with God, and he made that very clear to everyone around him. In that sense, I've tried to follow his lead.

However, he never used his faith as a battering ram, and I think that's especially important to look to as an example to follow in this particular chapter. He freely shared his own views, and focused on how his faith brought him hope, love and joy, but he never tried to force his views on his subordinates. When you left a conversation with Hondo Campbell you knew you had been with a great man of faith, but you never felt that he had rammed it down your throat. He simply shared what made him who he was: his relationship with God.

General Campbell was a four-star general, but he was an extremely humble man. He gave all glory to God and all thanks to his family. He regularly refused pomp and circumstance, a quality I also tried to emulate.

As a leader, when he came to visit, he truly came to help. Not all of our senior leaders in the Army did the same. I'm sure you're familiar with bosses who pop in looking for issues, almost as if they *want* to catch you doing something wrong. He was the opposite. He sincerely wanted to know how things were going, of course, but more importantly, he wanted to know what we needed. He wanted to help, and that sentiment was sincere.

I also knew that General Campbell had my best interests in mind. I always knew he would provide the "top cover" I needed in order to make tough calls and do the right things, even when some higher ups might have frowned upon it. He was such a blessing in that regard.

While he didn't ram his faith down anyone's throat, what he did do was always share his personal testimony, wherever he went. He believed that was what God wanted him to do.

Both on active duty and in retirement, General Campbell was always willing to speak at special events, and his faith was evident at all times.

He liked to cite Scripture, particularly Galatians 6:9:

> Let us not become weary in doing good, for at the proper time we will reap a harvest if we do not give up.

Every time I hear that verse I think of Hondo, and I always will.

There is power in doing good. The more good we do, the more the scales tip in favor of clean living—the more the pendulum swings away from our sinful nature.

Now, I can't say that Hondo Campbell wasn't a sinful guy. We're all sinful! I keep reminding myself of that, and hope you will too. Even if he was, it's not for any of us to judge. What I *can* say is that what I saw from him was an example of how to live the best life possible. He was what I refer to as a lifestyle evangelist. I never saw him get angry or upset. His calm demeanor was always a stabilizing influence in the room. He was able to sort through difficult issues and help us all arrive at workable solutions. His inner peace, which was a function of his relationship with God, was always evident.

I know people who worked with Hondo in Korea, where he was known for showing up every Sunday to the 8 a.m. Protestant service, which was not as well attended as the more conveniently timed 10:30 service. Despite his high position, there was never any fanfare. He and his wife came in quietly, took their seats in the pew, and participated in the service as regular parishioners. He always made a point to speak with everyone in the fellowship hall afterwards, too, particularly the Korean attendees. I'm not even sure if all of those people knew he was the Eighth Army Commander. He was simply a man living his faith, and demonstrating it quietly by example, which was always reassuring for the staff who attended that service.

Shortly after he arrived in Korea in November of 2002, there was a wave of strong anti-American feelings and protests triggered by the tragic, accidental deaths of two young Korean schoolgirls who were hit by one of our vehicles. Things got so bad, our service members were restricted to posts and bases as a safety measure. As the situation deteriorated and the protests grew more violent, *60 Minutes* came to Korea to do a story, and rather than put a spokesperson on camera or let some other subordinate take the heat, Hondo stepped up and did the interview himself. He was the commanding general, and he felt it was his responsibility to field the questions.

I know he drew on his faith to guide all U.S. forces through that rough time for the alliance. That inner faith and strength came through in his interview. When asked how he felt to watch the American flag get stomped on, burned, and dragged through the streets of Seoul, he gave an emotional, thoughtful response. He talked about what it meant to be a soldier and an American who had fought for that flag, and lost comrades defending what that flag stood for. It was powerful, and I have no doubt his heartfelt interview helped to quiet some of the rising tensions at the time.

The fact that Hondo was on TV and played such an important and public role in the Army was not the thing that mattered to his soldiers. What mattered is that he led with integrity and authenticity. He was the General who would stand in long lines, just like everybody else, in order to get his new military ID when he moved to a new base. He didn't have to. He could have had someone get it for him. He *chose* to stand with everyone else. He was the type of leader who would always remember the names of his subordinates' children; the type of leader who put a smile on everyone's face just by being around, and being so accessible.

I'm not sharing all of this to put General Campbell up on some pedestal. I'm sharing it because Hondo was the embodiment of the Scripture from Matthew 5:16:

> In the same way let your light shine before men, so they may see your good deeds and praise your Father in heaven.

He always did just that.

Hondo was also a man of strong personal convictions and amazing personal courage. He always did the right thing, for the right reasons, regardless of the consequences—living out that all-important part of the Cadet Prayer I've always admired: the ability to do the harder right rather than the easier wrong.

Just prior to his retirement, General Campbell was tasked to conduct the final investigation into the Battle of Wanat, Afghanistan, in which nine American Soldiers were killed and twenty-seven wounded by Taliban fighters in 2008. There had been a long probe into what went wrong that day, and there were those who believed senior leadership had been negligent in putting those soldiers into harm's way.

Campbell had initially determined that there *had* been negligence, and he decided to reprimand the chain of command.

But later, as a result of his own personal investigation and I am sure much prayer, he reversed his own decision and vindicated the chain of command instead. He was quoted as saying the investigation "must be focused on the totality of circumstances" that affected actions at Wanat. He also made it a point to emphasize the fact that "to criminalize command decisions in a theater of complex combat operations is a grave step indeed." He knew his decision would be unpopular and not well-received by family members of the soldiers who died that day, nor by some senior members of our Nation's leadership, but he did what he thought was right. Regardless of the pressure he was actively receiving, he stood by what he knew was the right thing to do—including admitting that he himself had been wrong in his initial finding.

That is demonstrated courage and strong moral character. I wish more of our leaders would show the same fortitude.

One of my favorite books is *A Life God Rewards* by Bruce Wilkinson. I am paraphrasing here, but my big takeaway from reading that book was that God really doesn't care now much money you make, or how many stars you wear on your uniform. God cares about how many people you touch. Did you truly live as a servant leader, trying every day to enrich the lives of the folks around you?

General Hondo Campbell surely did.

In Wilkinson's book, there is a graph that has a small dot connected by a line that goes out for all eternity. The small dot represents this thing called life, and the line shows us where we will be for eternity. The author highlights that we get into heaven based on our beliefs, but where we are in heaven is based on our behavior on earth.

In sharing that, I not only want to honor Hondo Campbell, but I hope I've held him up as one small example of how possible it is to lead a moral, courageous life in the name of God. In thinking about humble leaders in the last chapter, I asked you to think about not just general officers and Presidents, but sports figures, business leaders, and more. The point here is that those kinds of leaders, those who live life with the Faith of the Centurion, as Hondo Campbell did, those who bow before God and give Him all the glory are some of the very same leaders we can look to for inspiration on how to turn away from our evil ways.

These leaders, these human beings who've achieved greatness here on Earth that so many of us aspire to, have often done so while working hard at living in God's image, and praying hard for the guidance and forgiveness that only God provides.

Our Nation lost a great American and a National treasure when Muhammad Ali died on June 3, 2016. His fans called him "The Greatest," usually speaking of his boxing prowess, but I argue that he was also one of the "Greatest" when it came to his humanity and his love and concern for his fellow man. He was, without a doubt, a role model.

Ali started his boxing career at the age of twelve in Louisville, Kentucky, and continued until his retirement in 1981. At just eighteen years old, he won a gold medal in the 1960

Olympics. Then, as a pro, he had fifty-six wins—thirty-seven by knock out—and just five losses. He became the heavyweight champion of the world on three separate occasions.

As he so eloquently put it, he could "float like a butterfly and sting like a bee." But I think a lot of people would argue that his boxing career was on par with or maybe even eclipsed by his service to his fellow man. After all, Ali was acknowledged as an Ambassador for Peace in 1985 and nominated for the Nobel Peace Prize in 1987. He focused his efforts on service to others, stating, "Service to others is the rent you pay for your room here on earth." Imagine what would happen if more people emulated Ali in this regard?

While Muhammad wasn't a Christian, he was a very spiritual man. He became a member of the Nation of Islam in 1964, and in 1975 he became a Sunni Muslim. He believed that religions all have different names, but they all contain the same truths. He was accommodating when it came to different beliefs, because he knew there were certain truths common to all religions.

His life was not without controversy, though, nor was it without sin. He refused to be drafted at the age of twenty-six, citing religious reasons to forego military service. He was quoted as saying, "I ain't got no quarrel with those Viet Cong." He was stripped of his heavyweight title as a result of his refusal to fight. (That decision was overturned on appeal many years later.) He also fell into the same temptation as King and Kennedy when it came to women: he was known for having affairs during his marriages, and he was married four times.

Should any of that take away from his legacy? Should any of that cause any of us to judge him?

Ali inspired millions to do their very best, and he did it by personal example. He regularly reminded folks, "If my mind can conceive it and my heart can believe it, I can achieve it." He lived by a set of core principles, which included confidence, conviction, dedication, giving, respect, and spirituality; and he regularly declared, "The more we help others the more we help ourselves."

Those are all traits and beliefs that God rewards.

Despite his great gifts as an athlete and humanitarian, Ali was not without suffering. He was diagnosed with Parkinson's disease in 1984, and struggled with it for the last three decades of his life—but he never let the disease slow him down. He once stated, "He who is not courageous enough to take risks will accomplish nothing in life," and he demonstrated that by having the courage to continue leading a life of service to others right up until his death.

By most accounts, Muhammad Ali worked just as hard at being a great man as he worked at being a great boxer.

There's something each of us can learn from Ali: always do our very best; never let our circumstances get us down; always focus on serving our fellow man; stand up for our personal convictions; be a person of principle. If we do this, Ali's impact will continue for decades to come. If we instead choose to judge or dismiss him because of his sins, we will lose out on all of that great inspiration.

We cannot forget that the "heroes" and "role models" we look to are also human beings. They have flaws. They have *all* sinned. They have all faced challenges in life. They have all faced fear. They have all faced struggle and hardship.

Knowing that, the smart thing to do is to ask ourselves: How did they overcome? How did they manage to thrive when many others faltered? Where did they get their resiliency in life? How were they able to tap into the peace and praise that God brings? What was it they had in their kit bag that allowed them to turn away from evil?

In studying leadership, in studying history, in studying the Bible, and in trial and error through the course of the last thirty-plus years of my life, I can tell you the way it's done in just about every case is by developing a unique fitness routine that far too many of us are missing from our lives.

I'm not talking about going to the gym. I'm not talking about *physical* fitness here. What I'm talking about are the daily habits and rituals, the everyday routines we can add to our lives in order to develop the strongest kind of fitness of all. A fitness that builds resiliency. A fitness that builds character. A fitness that builds moral strength and a steadfast emotional foundation.

What I'm talking about here, and what I'll talk about for the length of the next chapter, is the key to unlocking the door to inner peace; the key to unlocking the power of everything you've read about in this book so far.

What I'm talking about is the act of developing something I call "Spiritual Fitness."

CHAPTER 6

Developing Spiritual Fitness

Three days after the motor pool blew up in Kuwait, tragedy struck.

The whole lot of us were still recovering from the shock of it all, feeling thankful that no one had died and just starting to clean up the colossal mess, when somebody accidentally tripped a wire on an unexploded ordinance in the motor pool.

We have some amazing weaponry in the Army, including mines that can be remotely fired into an area, arm themselves, and then lay in wait until the enemy comes along to trip them. Somehow, in the series of explosions in the motor pool, one of those mines managed to remain armed and unexploded; and somehow during the sweep of the area to make sure it was safe to walk through, that one stray mine got triggered.

The explosion killed three men. In one awful instant, three young soldiers were gone.

These are hazardous jobs we do in the Army. We all know the risks. Even though we weren't in active combat, the very nature of what we were doing there in Kuwait involved some level of danger at all times. But no one expected that explosion, just like no one expected the whole motor pool to go up in flames.

Enough was enough. With all we'd been through in those trying three days, I decided it was my job to save another soldier from having to go in and witness the sight of those three dead men. I could have sent someone else in to pick up the body parts, but I didn't. I took that task on myself, with just a couple other select individuals. I wanted to minimize the trauma and effect of that tragedy—out of respect to my men, both the living and the dead.

It was the not the first gruesome scene I had encountered up close in my military career, and it would not be the last.

I've participated in nearly every major combat operation the United States has been a part of since 1991, which means I've seen a lot. I've seen my men mortally wounded. I've had near brushes with death. I've been left with nothing but ringing in my ears because the explosions came so close, and seen shrapnel shred the bodies of soldiers I'd been talking to moments beforehand.

Back home, I've attended the funerals of hundreds of soldiers. I've stood side by side with family members whose hearts were so broken, just the sight of their faces could bring any man to tears.

I'm not unique in any of this. There are many of us in the Army who've done these things. Since the Gulf War, we've sent a couple million of our men and women into combat situations, and there are thousands of officers who've done the hard work of both offering support to and sometimes delivering the worst news of all to the families of our soldiers back home.

So I've asked myself: Why is it that some of us go off to war, witness horrible things, experience all sorts of trauma—including the loss of limbs in many cases—and come back with the ability to go on with our lives, some of us even feeling enriched by the experiences, while others go off and experience the very same things but return with horrible nightmares and other symptoms of PTSD, a debilitating set of invisible wounds that seem to knock us right out of the game? I'm not talking about Traumatic Brain Injury (TBI), which is a physical trauma caused by explosions, but rather the mental and spiritual wounds that as many as 200,000 soldiers seem to be suffering all across our land.

Why is it that Sarah has never had to calm me down from waking up screaming in the middle of the night, because I don't recall ever having a single nightmare related to my time in combat, when many wives experience that on a nightly basis with their husbands who've come home from the front lines? Why have I never experienced residual fear of loud noises, or been unable to function in any part of my daily life, when other soldiers and officers have experienced acute PTSD-type symptoms?

Outside of combat operations, in daily life, why is it that some people come through tragedies with more strength of character and resolve to work hard and change the world for the better, while others suffer and retreat—sometimes for the rest of their lives?

Is it just in our DNA? Or is the ability to survive and even thrive after enduring hardship something we can train ourselves to do? Is enduring tragedy and trauma something we can prepare ourselves for? Because unexpected traumas happen to all of us, whether we enlist in the Army or not. No matter how safe from it you may feel right this second, there is little doubt that it's coming—in some way, shape or form. I don't think there's a person on Earth who isn't affected by some awful shock at some point during their lifetime.

Figuring out how we prepare for the unexpected and the tragic, how we develop the ability to conduct ourselves in the middle of any situation that might unfold, and how we develop the fortitude to carry on in its wake—to me, seems like one of the most important discussions we ought to be having.

There seems to be lots of talk out there about how to treat trauma and depression. There are studies happening, there are new prescription medications being developed, there are always new methods of therapy going into practice, and many of those advances are having positive results. But as I've stepped back and looked at the course of my own life, especially after having the opportunity to study the effects of war on soldiers at the research institute I was in charge of after I transitioned out of the Army, I wonder why it is we're so focused on treatment after tragedy rather than trying to prepare for and get ahead of these tragedies in the first place.

I liken the difference between those two approaches to something we in the military refer to as "getting left of the boom."

In Iraq, one of the biggest plagues of the war was the proliferation of IEDs (Improvised Explosive Devices). The enemy was planting all kind of these things on the routes we traveled, and blowing up our trucks and personnel on a near daily basis at one point during the Iraq War. We seemed to have all sorts of response mechanisms in place for rescue and medical operations after an explosion occurred—or what we referred to as the time period "right of the boom"—but it occurred to some of us in the Army that what we really needed to do in order to stop this parade of trauma from happening was do everything in our power to get "left of the boom." We needed to better figure out how to detect and avoid run-ins with IEDs altogether; how to spot them and dismantle them and overcome them before we hit them.

I think it would do us all some good to get "left of the boom" in life, too, to better prepare ourselves for the IEDs that life will inevitably place in our paths.

I'm talking about the sort of things that came up at the very beginning of this book and have resurfaced at various points throughout: natural disasters (floods, tornadoes, hurricanes); human disasters (mass shootings, terrorist attacks, car accidents—and bus accidents); and even the smaller traumas that can sometimes affect us deeply, including the hiccups and delays in our fast-paced lives that lead many of us into bad behaviors. How are you going to handle the traffic jam that happens on the way to an important appointment? How are you going to handle the loss of your job? How are you going to handle the temptation of someone who wants you to cheat on your spouse? How are you going to handle the news that your mother or father has passed away? How are you going to handle the increase in your insurance premium, which you already can't afford? How are you going to handle the sudden loss of the one friend you could count on through thick and thin?

I can tell you how I used to handle some of these things: I'd get road rage, I'd rant and holler, I'd sometimes throw things, I'd sometimes break things. I was quick to fly off the handle throughout my twenties, and there are plenty of soldiers out there who were under my command who'd be happy to tell you all about it. My anger when somebody didn't do their job, especially if that job involved watching out for the safety of others, could be epic.

I still get angry at things, don't get me wrong. There're a whole lot of things in life that really tick me off. Especially the little annoyances in life. My children laugh at me every time we're in the car and I encounter someone blocking the right lane at an intersection. We allow right-turn-on-red in this country as a way to improve traffic flow, and when someone who is planning to go straight blocks that right lane at the stop light rather than moving into the center lane, it just gets under my skin. How can they show that much lack of consideration for all the cars behind them?

Thankfully as I've gotten older, and hopefully a little wiser (thanks to the principles I'm spending so much time talking about in this book), I've found that anger doesn't consume me. Just as worry doesn't consume me. Just as fear doesn't consume me. Just as sadness doesn't consume me.

Case in point: I lost my father as I was writing this book. My relationship with my father was strained for pretty much all my life. He was hard on me. Even after I became an adult, a fully-grown man, a father and grandfather myself, he had a way of saying things that would cut me right down. It made me angry every time he did it. But I didn't let that anger keep me from seeing him now and then. I didn't let that anger block me from recognizing that he was my dad, and that somewhere deep down in all of the issues he had, he loved me. He cared about me. That's why he used his belt to keep me in line and push me through school, which helped me to achieve everything I've achieved in my life.

Losing him was sad. It was unexpected. He was old, sure, but I'd just seen him not long before it happened, and he seemed to be in pretty good health. So it was shocking, and I'll be sorting out the emotions of all of it for a long time to come. But his death didn't stop me. It didn't keep me from finishing this book and continuing to focus on my kids and my grandchildren, and my marriage, and the blessings of the good life I've been busy building for Sarah and myself here in Texas since I transitioned out of the military.

The death of my father was a trauma that, like it or not, I was well prepared to handle. And the reason I was able to get through it is the very same reason I don't express much road rage anymore, even when I have somewhere important to go; the same the reason I've been able to stop getting so angry at most of life's little hiccups; the exact same reason I'm able to sleep peacefully at night without constantly reliving the horrors of war in my mind; and the same reason I've been able to stay faithful to my wife and happily married for so many decades now despite all the friction that comes with marriage.

I'm living the way we're told to live in the Bible, in as many ways as possible, including in the way professed in James 1:19:

> My dear brothers and sisters, take note of this: Everyone should be quick to listen, slow to speak, and slow to become angry,

How am I able to do that? What it all comes down to is the fact that for more than thirty years now, I've been doing the hard work it takes to get "left of the boom."

The Gift of Daily Habits

Spiritual Fitness isn't something that happens in an instant. Like physical fitness, it is something that gets easier, grows better and makes you stronger in time. And what it really comes down to—just like diet and exercise—are the daily rituals and habits that change you and come to define your life for the better.

My personal Spiritual Fitness routine begins every morning when I get out of bed and start my day in prayer. I mentioned a bit about how to pray in the last chapter, following the acronym "A.C.T.S." It's a pretty simple thing to do: to wake up, acknowledge God's greatness (A), confess your sins (C), give thanks (T), and do a little supplication by asking for the blessings you want to receive (S). It's a ritual that helps you focus on what's important by defining what you want and what you don't want in your life, coupled with a humble acknowledgement that God is always above you. Just by performing that one simple act, you're starting your day by striving to live with the Faith of the Centurion. And that's a pretty good place to start.

I follow that up with some Bible study. As it's stated in Joshua 1:8:

> Keep this Book of the Law always on your lips; meditate on it day and night, so that you may be careful to do everything written in it. Then you will be prosperous and successful.

I don't know about you, but the idea of being "prosperous and successful" sounds pretty good to me. So that is why I meditate and study the Bible, and do my best to memorize many of its words—day and night.

If that sounds like too much of a chore to you, all I can say is this: It isn't. It's not a chore at all. It's a gift.

First of all, Bible study doesn't have to take too long. You don't have to spend hours and hours just to get started. And today, there are all sorts of websites and apps out there that can help you to do it. I used to just pick up my Bible and read a bit in the mornings, but today I use a website called OurDailyBread.org, which provides a new Bible lesson every morning. It only takes me a few minutes to read, and yet it provides me with a reminder of just how powerful the Bible is.

Rather than waking up and thinking about nothing but work or chores or the daily things that can easily consume us, that little timeout to think about God's word helps me keep in mind that I need not be so concerned about the little things that tend to overwhelm. It's also astounding just how often something I'll read in one of those daily Bible studies will align with an issue I'm having or some problem I'm facing, and will wind up setting my mind at ease.

In fact, there are times when I am convinced that the Our Daily Bread entry is initially blank, and God fills it in that morning depending on what you need that day. For example, as I was struggling to determine exactly what my second book should be about, God showed me the way through the Daily Bread. My writer, Mark Dagostino, and I were working our way through the potential structure of the book, initially focused on the idea of "having" the Faith of the Centurion. That day, as I was doing my Bible study, the scripture was James 2:17:

> Faith by itself, if it is not accompanied by action, is dead.

I shared that scripture with Mark, and the book took a turn from "having the faith" to "living the faith." It is what led us to the idea of "the power of faith in action," and led us to the discussion of James Marsh and his "work hard, pray hard" mantra.

I am convinced it was a message from God.

In fact, every day as I was working through some aspect of this book, the Daily Bread entry and my other scripture readings seemed to focus exactly on what I needed. Another example: I was editing Chapter 7 on "Trusting God," and the scripture that popped up was Psalm 20:7:

> Some trust in chariots and some in horses, but we trust in the name of the Lord our God.

This isn't a recent thing with me. Even in combat in Iraq I turned to Our Daily Bread to begin my day. Numerous scriptures were presented to me at exactly the right time, just when I needed them the most.

One morning in 2007 during the Surge, as I began my day in prayers, the Bible verse I was presented with was Joshua 1:9, reminding me to not be terrified and not be discouraged for the Lord our God would be with me wherever I went.

Immediately after I finished my Bible study I received a call from my operations center informing me that one of our platoons had been ambushed; several Soldiers had been killed or wounded, and three had been taken captive.

Having Joshua 1:9 on my mind that day was exactly what I needed.

I could give you a hundred examples, but go try it out and chances are you'll see what I mean for yourself.

I'll admit I was resistant to sitting down and reading the Bible when I first got started. I only tried it because I was so desperate to find some inner peace, and I really wanted to succeed. Joe Miller gave me assignments and I didn't want to fail. Fear of failure can be a pretty good motivator at times. But the thing I learned pretty quickly is that I enjoyed it. I enjoyed reading the Bible, deciphering some of the language, stumbling across lines that resonated with me and passages that seemed to talk about the things I was going through in my own life. I even enjoyed some of the rote memorization of Scripture. Having those lines that resonated with me right there on my tongue when I needed them, when I wanted to make a point to somebody or when I needed to remind myself of something, just felt good.

As it says in 2 Timothy 3:16:

> All Scripture is God-breathed and is useful for teaching, rebuking, correcting and training in righteousness,

Perhaps it also feels good because God smiles on those who do it. There's a passage about that, where God refers to one group of people who study the Bible daily as being "of more noble character" than those who don't. It's in Acts 17:11:

> Now the Berean Jews were of more noble character than those in Thessalonica, for they received the message with great eagerness and examined the Scriptures every day to see if what Paul said was true.

I didn't continue to read the Bible because I felt "more noble" than anyone else. Like I said, it just felt good to do, and so it quickly became a habit. And habits—the good as well as the bad—have a powerful effect in our lives. I think you know how bad habits hurt you, and how hard they can be to break, whether it's smoking cigarettes, or overeating, or drinking too much alcohol, or even just being lazy and watching TV too much when you know you should be out doing something else. But let's not focus on that right now. Let's focus on the more positive habits that you might not even think about a whole lot, because they're just a part of who you are.

What are some of the things you do every morning? Do you stretch? Do you walk outside and get the paper? Do you run? Do you make a big pot of your favorite brand of coffee?

Do you immediately hop in the shower so you feel refreshed and ready to go? Do you brush your teeth first thing?

I know this will be hard to remember, but guess what? There was a time when you didn't do any of those things. There was a time before any of those little habits were habits. But you started doing whatever it is you do, and you kept doing it, and before long it was such a part of your routine that it now feels weird when you *don't* do whatever that ritual is. Am I right?

Breaking habits can be hard, but making new habits is actually kind of easy. You just start doing whatever it is you want to do and repeat that action until it starts to feel routine. Running a few miles every day is a great example. Just ask anyone who's managed to add that routine to his or her life. Yes, it takes some hard work and serious effort and motivation, but the payoff is huge. People feel better once they make it a habit, and even those who don't think they can pull it off find they can if they're motivated to lose that weight or get in shape and change their lives.

Running's a big deal. It's hard at first. And I'm not asking you to even think about doing something that hard. What I'm suggesting is that doing a little Bible study, when there are websites and apps designed to help you, doesn't take much effort at all. And if you experience anything like I've experienced, or anything like so many people who do this on a daily basis experience, you'll find that adding this one simple habit to your routine makes a difference in your life—just as the Bible tells you it will.

And when that habit of Bible study is coupled with the habit of praying on a regular basis, too, it's powerful. It's as powerful as all of the examples I've shared in this book so far. So go back and look for your inspiration. Is it General Robert E. Lee? Or Ulysses S. Grant? Or maybe it's Stonewall Jackson, or George Patton. Maybe it's a sports figure, like Tom Landry. Maybe it's the countless soldiers who've come through war with their spirits and souls intact. Or maybe it's the Centurion himself. Perhaps it's someone in your own circle of friends and associates whom you've come to admire. Whomever it is, wherever you find that inspiration, look at the amazing things that have happened in his or her life, and how much of that success and prosperity they truly believe was brought about wholly because of their daily prayers to and meditations on God and the Bible. Those inspirational figures aren't lying! They're trying to give you the message. They're trying to share with you, with me, with all of us, just how powerful it is to keep God in your corner through the daily habits and routines of developing your Spiritual Fitness.

Now, some of you may have been raised to think that the only way to stay in touch with God and live a faithful life is by going to church on Sunday. That may have been the only notion of "Spiritual Fitness" you've ever had, and you may have a good reason why you stopped going, or never went in the first place, or don't want to go to church now. I've struggled with this one, and I have to say I don't have all the answers on this subject. (I hope you understand by now I don't claim to have all the answers about any of this. Only

God has all the answers. But we'll get to more of that in the next chapter.)

What I *can* say about the idea of going to church is that, just like any of this, the decision on how you worship, how you pray, how you go about achieving your Spiritual Fitness in general is up to you. And I really do think the part in the Bible that tells us not to judge is more important than ever in this chaotic modern world in which we live. You may have noticed that I haven't professed to support any one branch of Christian church in this book; in fact, I have avoided it very purposefully. I can't say whether one branch of Christian faith is better than another, and as a Christian it's not my place to condemn anyone who is outside of the Christian faith, either. Faith in God is what's important. The common core principles professed across almost all religions are what matter the most. And when it comes to the subject of going to one particular church or another, or not going to church at all, I believe that is up to each individual to decide for himself or herself.

This subject came up in a very famous "Letter from God."

It's funny how we put so much emphasis on miracles and messages received hundreds or even a couple of thousand years ago, when there are new messages sent to us all the time. One of those messages was read by the famous radio personality Paul Harvey, in 1998. According to Paul, who had been on radio for years and had an extremely popular syndicated news show on radio stations all across the country at that time, he walked into his office one day and found a letter on his desk. The letter said it was from God! He thought it was a joke at first, or a hoax, but he sat down and read it, and the letter moved him deeply. He still wasn't sure if someone had written it and just signed it "God," and that made him nervous. He struggled for six weeks or so before he finally decided to go ahead and read the letter on the air—and the letter became a sensation. People all over the country were moved and touched by it, and in some cases angered by it. It blew up into a media sensation, even in those days before the sensationalizing power of social media.

I've done some reading on this letter, and there has never been any evidence that Paul Harvey wrote it himself, nor that someone else wrote it besides God. Today, you can find the reading of the letter on YouTube and other places on the Internet, and it's worth a read or listen, for sure. It's astounding how strongly the words in that letter resonate today as much as they did in the late 1990s. The message is timeless, which is another reason people wonder if God Himself delivered it.

Regardless, the point I want to make is about churches and religions. In a section of the "Letter from God" that Paul Harvey read, God says:

> "You see, one human being to me, even a bum on the street, is worth more than all of the holy books in the world. That's just the kind of a guy I am. My spirit is not an historical thing. It's alive right here, right now, as fresh as your next breath.
>
> "Holy books and religious rites are sacred and powerful, but they are not more so than the least of you. They were only meant to steer you in the right direction, not to keep you arguing with each other and certainly not to keep you from trusting your own personal connection with me.

> "Which brings me to my next point about your nonsense. You act like I need you and your religions to stick up for me or win souls for my sake. Please, don't do me any favors. I can stand quite well on my own, thank you. I don't need you to defend me. I don't need constant credit. I just want you to be good to each other."

I took that message to heart, and ever since I heard it I've done my best not to judge anyone in any way based on what church they choose to go to, or not to go to.

I personally struggled with the idea of going to church even after I was baptized. Sarah and I were still extremely busy, and Sundays were often our one day to rest. The idea of dragging myself out of bed for some early morning sermon just didn't sit well with me. Plus, with the moves to Germany and then Kuwait, the standard ideas of weekly routines got blown out of the water anyway. I only started going to church regularly once I was back in the States, in the mid-1990s. I made a habit of it, which continues to this day. That is my choice, and I'll explain why momentarily.

The thing is, I've confronted the issue of going to church within my own family: my daughter, like a lot of Millennials, won't go to church anymore. She won't go to church even though she was raised going most Sundays, and even though she's a strong believer. She'll show up for special occasions, like the baptism of her nephew or something, but while I was working on this book we learned that she and her husband were expecting a baby—and she made it perfectly clear she doesn't want her daughter baptized in a church. She wants me to baptize her daughter instead, which is flattering, and isn't contrary to anything in my belief system. Avoiding the pomp and circumstance seems like a humble thing to do, and the Bible doesn't say that you have to be an ordained minister to baptize somebody, so I plan on granting her wish when the time comes.

It seems as if my daughter isn't alone in this. Millennials as a whole have great questioning minds about the idea of going to church and listening to people preach about things you might not believe. On those times when my daughter does go to church with us, she'll usually leave aggravated because the pastor said something she doesn't believe in. And I've tried to explain to her, "Hey, the pastor is not somebody who's out speaking exactly what God wants you to hear. He's speaking *his* view of what God says, *his* interpretation. And you may agree with it or you may not agree with it. That's okay."

I've also asked my daughter, "Why do you think I go to church?"

The reason I ask her is because I want to remind her of my answer: I go to church because it's an hour of focus on God. Even during my morning prayer most days, something will distract me. There'll be a calendar issue I'll have to deal with, or a text message that'll pop up. But that one hour in church, once a week, where the cell phone is turned off and nobody's asking me questions, allows me to do nothing but stay focused on God. *That's* the reason I go to church.

I don't go because I feel the need for some pastor to lead me to God—although I did in the beginning, of course. I don't go because I need somebody to help interpret Scripture for me. I don't need somebody to lead me in prayer. Through my own Spiritual Fitness routine, I'm able to do all of those things for myself now. So that's not why I go to church. I go to church to give myself that guaranteed single hour of focus each week. If something comes up and I can't make it, I don't feel guilty about it. I don't wake up on a Sunday and say, "If I don't go to church, God's going to be mad at me." I'm pretty sure God's not keeping an attendance ledger.

There are passages in the Bible that talk about gathering believers together, but I think those passages are pretty open to interpretation. We gather together with other Christians in all sorts of ways. We even gather together on our Facebook pages, don't we? I believe there are benefits that come from surrounding ourselves with like-minded people, people who've developed a trust in God, as there's power in teamwork. Through teamwork it's possible for people to lift each other up and support each other in all sorts of ways. But I cannot argue that participating in an organized church is necessary to developing Spiritual Fitness. And it's the development of that Spiritual Fitness, which leads you to having a personal relationship with God, which is the most important thing of all.

As it says in 1 Timothy 4:7-11:

> Have nothing to do with godless myths and old wives' tales; rather, train yourself to be godly. For physical training is of some value, but godliness has value for all things, holding promise for both the present life and the life to come. This is a trustworthy saying that deserves full acceptance. That is why we labor and strive, because we have put our hope in the living God, who is the Savior of all people, and especially of those who believe.

Prayer, Bible study, going to church—these can all become part of your Spiritual Fitness routine. Or not. Maybe there're other ways to go about this. It's up to each one of us to find the routines that work for us, and are comfortable for us. What I've found is when those routines are comfortable enough that they become habits, they become so much a part of who you are that you don't even have to think about doing them. When that happens, your Spiritual Fitness builds strength over time, the same way you build muscles and endurance in the gym or out on the track.

No matter how you look at it or how you approach it, spending some time every day developing habits that strengthen your Spiritual Fitness are important.

But that's not where Spiritual Fitness ends. If you want it to work for you, you then have to go out and share it.

Lifestyle Evangelism

In my leadership book *Adapt or Die*, I talked a lot about "lifestyle evangelism," which is basically the idea that you should set a good example for the people you lead. What better leaders are there than those who lead by example? Who better to follow than someone who makes you want to get up and do the things they do, so you, too, can get ahead in life and accomplish great things?

That same concept is just as effective in life as it is in work—and, not surprisingly, the Bible addresses this idea directly. The very same passage from 1 Timothy 4 that I referenced above goes on to tell us how important it is to share our faith, to share our knowledge, at any age, in 1 Timothy 4:12–16:

> Command and teach these things. Don't let anyone look down on you because you are young, but set an example for the believers in speech, in conduct, in love, in faith, and in purity. Until I come, devote yourself to the public reading of Scripture, to preaching, and to teaching. Do not neglect your gift, which was given you through prophecy when the body of elders laid their hands on you.
>
> Be diligent in these matters; give yourself wholly to them, so that everyone may see your progress. Watch your life and doctrine closely. Persevere in them, because if you do, you will save both yourself and your hearers.

I've already mentioned the phrase from Tom Landry that resonated so strongly with me: "Being a Christian isn't about who you are, it's about what you do." What this passage from 1 Timothy tells us is what we *ought to do*, as Christians, is to share our faith with others by setting a strong example.

I personally think some folks interpret this 1 Timothy directive a little too fervently. I'm not sure there's all that much value in standing on a box on a street corner, preaching to the crowds of mostly annoyed people who are just trying to get on about their work or their shopping trips. You can't be a "green-toothed Christian," as Joe Miller so eloquently put it to me. You don't want to be that Christian that turns people off and no one wants to listen to. But preaching and teaching in a more personal way, to those around us, to friends, to family, to coworkers, simply through being a good Christian, being humble, being compassionate, and then having the ability to answer questions (when asked) by quoting Scripture—that to me seems like something that's both good and easy to do as you build your Spiritual Fitness.

Again, it's about what you do—and one of the things Christians do is lead people to Christ.

I've found that many Christians are uncomfortable sharing their faith. I call them "Closet Christians" because they hide their Christianity and their beliefs. When I ask them why, they tell me two primary reasons: one is that they know they sin and they don't want to be hypocritical; another is that they don't know the Bible well enough.

First I remind them: "We all sin and fall short of the Glory of God. That's Romans 3:23. Everyone sins! The key is to acknowledge our sins and confess our sins, and then try to do better each and every day." (Now that I've written this book, maybe I'll just direct them to Chapter 5.)

I love to remind people that the only person who came close to being perfect died for our sins on the cross. So don't let your sinful nature keep you in the closet.

Second, I tell them to study the Bible, even a little bit. Try to do it every day. Memorize some scripture. Use it to share your personal testimony. It takes some time and effort, but that time and effort is well worth it.

"Come out of the closet!" I say. "Tell folks about how your personal relationship with God gets you through difficult times. Share the 'Good News.' You'll be glad you did."

Once people go out and actually read the Bible, of course, they find that the twelve apostles were the primary disciples of Jesus. They were the teachers of the gospel, in a very direct way, after Jesus sent them on the Great Commission, as discussed in Matthew 28:19:

> "Therefore go and make disciples of all nations, baptizing them in the name of the Father and of the Son and of the Holy Spirit, and teaching them to obey everything I have commanded you. And surely I am with you always, to the very end of the age."

I believe that message was meant for all of us, and I really took it to heart when I took command of the tank battalion at Fort Hood. I was finally in a position of leadership, so I started a series of weekly Bible studies on base. I also started monthly prayer breakfasts where I'd invite guests to come in and speak. I built upon those activities with each promotion. It was at one of the prayer breakfasts I put together as a Brigade Commander where Tom Landry made such an impression on me. And later, as Corps Commander, I went so far as to set up a non-denominational Spiritual Fitness Center at Fort Hood, where anyone who needed a lift could come and get some guidance and support without judgment or being preached at in some overbearing way.

Yet the biggest part of what I've done to live up to the directive the Apostles received—that we've all received—has been to try to show by example that I'm living a life God wants me to live.

As it says in Matthew 5:16:

> In the same way, let your light shine before others, that they may see your good deeds and glorify your Father in heaven.

It really is that simple. That's all you need to do in order to see your Spiritual Fitness grow. If you're doing your best and working hard to live a life that God wants you to live, it's just a matter of letting your light shine before others—so they can see it, and hopefully develop a desire to exude that kind of light themselves.

It's a cliché line from a movie, but it's that whole idea of, "If you build it, they will come." That notion is certainly a part of the positive effect of building up your Spiritual Fitness and living life with the Faith of the Centurion. People are drawn to it. They will see how you're doing in life, and they'll ask about it. They'll want to know where you get your strength, where you get your courage, where you get your perseverance, where you get your resilience—all of these things. I get asked these sorts of things all the time, and I've grown more than comfortable with sharing what I believe. It's a joy to share these things with others, which is part of the reason I wanted to write this book.

What I'm uncomfortable doing, though, is telling others how *they* should believe. That's not me. I would rather show them through my own example, and know that I have answers for them about what's worked for me.

I assure you that after doing all of this daily Spiritual Fitness work, whatever that work should be in your case, you'll have answers for them too.

Of course, all of this is easier said than done, right?

It's not always easy to maintain good habits. Trying to live a life in God's image is not as simple as saying that you want to live a life in God's image. It takes hard work. It takes prayer. (Let's not forget James Marsh's words and the title of this book.)

But it also takes something else: It takes help.

You Can't Do This Alone

Back in Chapter 5, when talking about the importance of overcoming our sinful nature, I was reluctant to open up about too many of my personal sins from the past. The way I see it, those sins are between God and me. But I think it's important to acknowledge a little bit more about who I was back in my twenties in order to understand the point I'm aiming to make here.

When I was a young Captain in the Army, and single, I followed a pretty reliable daily routine. After work every day, I put fifty dollars in my wallet and I'd go out drinking and carousing. I'd only come home when I ran out of money. I would regularly wind up closing down the bar at two in the morning, even during the weekdays, and even though I had to be in my office at six in the morning to run PT with my soldiers. So I'd run PT with my soldiers and come back and sleep on my couch until it was time to go to work. My first sergeant would wake me up.

I kept doing all this silly stuff, things I never should have done, drinking and carousing and all that. It was fun, but it was also a pretty empty pursuit. I knew deep down I wanted more out of life than wasting all my time and money in bars, but at the time I didn't see a reason to stop.

And then, all of a sudden, in the summer of 1982, I met Sarah.

At one point during those single years, I had made a checklist of all of the qualities I wanted in a wife. And Sarah was the embodiment of every one of those qualities.

After I pursued her over a fairly long period of time (she kept refusing to go out with me, because her parents told her to never date a G.I.), we finally went on our first date. Sarah was a bodybuilder at the time, so it didn't take long before I saw her in a bikini. And she looked *good*. I admit that I fell in lust—but it wasn't long before I fell in love. And the more I got to know her, the more I knew I wanted to marry her.

Our first date was in July. I proposed in October, and we got married in December—and thirty-three years later, we're still cooking.

When I look back on it now and think about the checklist I made citing the qualities my future wife would have, I wonder if God heard that as a prayer. Even though I wasn't going to church or reading the Bible or living humbly, was making that list an act of prayer in God's eyes? Because He sure did answer it.

Once Sarah was in my life, the drinking and carousing routine went out the window. It just plain stopped. I wanted to be with Sarah, fully and completely, and I was. I really do credit Sarah's presence with putting an end to that more sinful part of my life. But my carousing lifestyle wasn't the only thing she helped me with.

I attempted to resign from the Army on four separate occasions. I was fed up and angry and bitter and felt like the only way things were going to get better was if I quit. But Sarah didn't let me. She talked me off the proverbial ledge each time.

I mentioned earlier that she encouraged me to stick it out when I wanted to quit MIT. She was there for me, encouraging me to do the right thing—which is not always the easy thing—and to step back and look at my life from a broader perspective, rather than getting bogged down in the immediacy of my frustrated situation.

When I look back on it now, I am wholly convinced that God sent Sarah to me to keep me out of trouble; and I am absolutely convinced He sent her to me to try to get me back on some kind of a righteous path.

It worked.

Making the right choices in life can be hard, and if there's one thing I've learned looking back on my life, it's that none of us can do this alone. We all need guidance. We all need encouragement. We all need someone in our lives who can help us along the way.

Turns out there's a figure in the Bible who proves this point well, and his name is Barnabas—a name that literally means "son of encouragement." He was a charismatic leader who focused his entire life on helping others. He's the guy who introduced Paul to the Apostles, and was described as "one who dedicated his life to the Lord."

Barnabas was self-sacrificing. For instance, at one point Barnabas sold a field that he owned and gave the money to the Apostles. He made the ultimate sacrifice in the name of Christ, too, as he was stoned to death for preaching the gospel. (It's interesting to note that all but one of the original disciples was martyred. John, the disciple that Jesus loved, died of old age; and Judas committed suicide after betraying Jesus. There's a lot to be learned from each of their lives, and the sacrifices they made in the name of God, especially since Jesus told His disciples at the outset that their work would entail great sacrifice. Yet, each of them went forward in doing the Lord's work anyway. They stepped up. They volunteered. They did what each of us is expected to do, as revealed in Isaiah 6:8:

> Then I heard the voice of the Lord saying, "Whom shall I send? And who will go for us?"
> And I said, "Here am I. Send me!"

But I don't want to stray too far from the topic at hand here, which is focusing on the example of Barnabas, the encourager.

The self-sacrificing way in which Barnabas lived his life was just as the Bible says all believers are supposed to live, as described in Acts 4:32-36:

> All the believers were one in heart and mind. No one claimed that any of their possessions was their own, but they shared everything they had. With great power the apostles continued to testify to the resurrection of the Lord Jesus. And God's grace was so powerfully at work in them all that there were no needy persons among them. For from time to time those who owned land or houses sold them, brought the money from the sales and put it at the apostles' feet, and it was distributed to anyone who had need.

Some people might look at that passage and think it sounds like communism or socialism, or think about the "no possessions" line from John Lennon's song "Imagine." But I see it instead as laying out what a good encourager like Barnabas ought to do in life: (1) Meet the needs of others, (2) Pray for the people, and (3) Build up people with direct words of encouragement.

What I came to realize in my Christian walk is that Sarah is, and always has been, my Barnabas.

Every time I tried to leave the army, every time I tried to quit MIT, every time I've faced a difficult decision in my life, she has been there encouraging and supporting me. That's why I like to thank her in my speeches. I realize I could not have accomplished what I've accomplished in life without her sacrifice and encouragement, and the same can be said of any service member. In fact, the next time you see a service member and his or her family out at a restaurant, go up and thank the service member for his or her service, but also thank the family—because they were the ones supporting that individual in what he or she was doing for our nation. The services and the sacrifices of the families often going unnoticed, and they shouldn't, because they are indeed helping the modern-day Centurions to live up to their potential.

In my particular case, as I tried to live the Faith of the Centurion of the last three-plus decades, I know I couldn't have done it had it not been for Sarah helping me. When I needed support, she was there to support me. When I needed a good kick in the behind, she was there to do that too.

As I built my daily habits of Spiritual Fitness, it became clear to me just how important her role was; and today, whenever I'm faced with something difficult in my life, I do two things. First, I stop and pray. Second, I go talk to Sarah. I say, "What do we do here? What do you think?" And I listen to her counsel, which is sometimes in sharp contrast to whatever it is I'm thinking, because I know her words inevitably help lead me toward the best decision. Quite honestly, I don't know how I would have made it in *life* without her by my side, encouraging me every step of the way.

I think it's important to ask: Who is your Barnabas? Who is your encourager? Who is the person helping you? Because you cannot do this alone.

Who is that person providing you the support you need, so in difficult times, in addition to your faith, there's somebody there to act as back up for you?

Also, on a day-to-day basis, who is the Barnabas in your life who holds you accountable?

When it comes to Spiritual Fitness, your Barnabas can be like your running partner, your workout coach, that person who's there to keep you going when you think you want to give up. That's important. And don't be limited by thinking you can only have one Barnabas in your life, either. You can have a number of Barnabases if you so choose. It's up to you.

I've attended a number of Promise Keepers events over the years. Promise Keepers is a men's Christian organization founded by Bill McCartney back when he was the head football coach at the University of Colorado–Boulder. (The whole idea of creating an organization that helped men build stronger relationships with Christ began during a conversation he had with a man named Dave Wardell, and I actually had the good fortune of bringing Wardell in for one of my prayer luncheons at Fort Hood. He was certainly an inspirational guy, and showed himself as a great encourager to McCartney during the whole foundation of what Promise Keepers is all about.) It was at those Promise Keepers events where I learned a lot about having accountability partners in life—people around you who remind you that you're not nearly as good as you think you are, and who tell you that maybe you ought to work a little bit harder. So while Sarah is the major Barnabas in my life, I do have accountability partners and promise keepers with me as well, and we promise to hold each other accountable.

Of course in turn, that means I'm acting as a Barnabas to others too. Being an encourager and receiving encouragement go hand in hand when "all the believers [are] one in heart and mind."

Getting to the Top of the Stairs

Adding Spiritual Fitness to your daily routine might not seem to make an overwhelming difference in your life right away. You might not feel it. You might not even notice a change. But take it from me: that is no reason to give up.

Think of it like doing sit-ups every day, or taking a walk every day. You might go about it for a while and think, "Hey, I'm not really losing all that much weight," or "I'm not seeing a dramatic enough physical change on the outside of my body to bother keeping this up." But then one day you climb a set of stairs and you realize that for the first time in years, you're not completely winded when you reach the top. You've changed. Your body is different. It's healthier. It's more at ease.

That is the feeling you get when you work on your Spiritual Fitness.

When the next stress comes, when the tragedy happens, when the unexpected news comes flooding in, you will find there is a power and a resiliency inside of you that is greater than anything you have ever known.

Once you've had that experience at the top of the staircase, how can you ever go back? Sure, you may backslide in your fitness routines now and then, but even when you do, chances are you're going to get back on that saddle and start exercising again, because you've developed a knowledge that you didn't have before you started exercising. (And if you're doing this right, you've got a Barnabas there to encourage you to pick up your fitness routine again too.) You trust in the fact that exercise yields results. You trust in knowing that the hard work you put in at the gym, or out pounding the pavement, or at the yoga studio, or on your bike, is going to make you feel better: freer, lighter, healthier, more alive.

It's amazing how a Spiritual Fitness routine will do the same thing for your spirit, your mind, your heart, and your soul.

At some point you'll trust that what you're doing will *always* yield results.

And through that trust, a Spiritual Fitness routine will help lead you to the most important thing of all: Trust in God.

CHAPTER 7

Trusting God

You've reached the seventh chapter. It's no coincidence that this is the seventh and most important step in the journey of faith. The number "7" plays a significant role in the Bible. It signifies completeness and perfection, both physical and spiritual. It is used 735 times in the Bible, and is tied directly to God's creation (since the Sabbath day is the 7th day). The Bible has 7 major divisions, and 49 inspired books (7 × 7). There were 7 miracles performed by Jesus. The Book of Revelation talks to 7 churches, 7 angels, and 7 seals. Jesus tells 7 parables in the Book of Matthew.

Thanks to all of that, I tend to notice the number 7 in life nowadays. I don't think the number itself has any sort of magical powers or anything. I just think that anything that is shown such great significance in the Bible is something we ought to pay attention to, and when I think back to the fact that Walter and Peggy Price—the very first people who took me to church and tried to lead me to Jesus—lived at 777 Fairhaven Drive, it sure makes me wonder. There was certainly great significance to that couple and what they did for me, helping me to dip my toe into Christianity for the first time ever, and at this point, I see no reason *not* to believe that their street number was some sort of a sign from God.

Come to think of it, there isn't much I question about God today at all. I believe in God, and I trust that His infinite wisdom is something far greater than anything my finite mind can imagine.

Believing in that infinite wisdom—trusting in it, knowing it is there, being absolutely positive that it is real—is freeing.

It is because of that trust that I am not anxious. About anything.

In Chapter 1, I talked about my desire for "inner peace," and how I started down the road to finding inner peace through my baptism. I also mentioned what I find to be one of the most inspiring pieces of Scripture anywhere in the Bible, Philippians 4: 6-7:

> Do not be anxious about anything, but in every situation, by prayer and petition, with thanksgiving, present your requests to God. And the peace of God, which transcends all understanding, will guard your hearts and your minds in Christ Jesus.

I didn't really get it when I first started my Christian walk. I wanted to. I tried to. But it took me nearly thirty years to work through all the steps it takes to get to a point where I truly felt the power that particular passage delivers.

I hope this book will help others to get there a little quicker.

When I first learned that the peace of God could be the answer I was seeking, I think I got it backwards. I thought by getting closer to God—by praying, by giving thanks— that my anxiety would go away. I thought it was sort of an A plus B equals C kind of equation. But if you look at the passage more carefully, what it says to do *first* is "Do not be anxious about anything." That's the first thing that's supposed to happen, not the last. *Then*, through prayer and petition and thanksgiving, the Peace of God will come.

It's a small distinction on the surface, but it really is important. In fact, it's reiterated in Psalms 46:10:

> Be still, and then you will know that I am God

In some translations, including this God's Word translation, Psalm 46:10 is interpreted even more plainly:

> Let go of your concerns!
> Then you will know that I am God.

It doesn't say, "Get to know God, and then God will relieve you of your concerns." It doesn't say, "Know God first and then God will let you be still and at peace." It's the other way around!

It is through the *act* of letting go of our concerns, through the *act* of not being anxious, through the *act* of putting our faith first and knowing that God is in charge of all things, that we get to know the true peace that God brings.

There's a phrase that's been popularized by people like Pastor Rick Warren that sums up what this is all about: "Let Go, Let God."

After thirty years of trying, this is exactly where I am in my life today. In all things, I trust that God has control, and that God is going to lead me where I need to go. I finally realized that every day I'm going to be confronted by things beyond my control. *Every day.* It's predictable that when you go to bed, regardless of how many things you put on your list to do the next day, something is going to happen that will cause you to have to shift your priorities. The only reliable thing is that there will be circumstances beyond your control.

It could be the weather, it could be somebody else's schedule, it could be traffic, it could be a sudden terrorist attack, it could be anything—big or small. The thing is, as human beings, there is little that we can control. We cannot control the weather, and we can't control what other people think and choose to do, or how they drive, or whom they hate, no matter how much we try. We're not God!

What I've come to grips with over the last thirty years is when those circumstances arise, the first thing I do is stop and I pray. I let go and let God. I turn it over to God and say, "God, these circumstances as you well know are here right in front of me. This is what I'm trying to deal with. Please give me your insight. Show me the direction. Give me some sense as to how I should deal with this." From there I'm comfortable that God is going to show me the way.

I know He's not going to ring me up on my cell phone and say, "Rick, this is God. I heard your question. Here's the answer." But He is going to send something my way to cause me to go left or right, and I'm very, very, comfortable with trusting that.

Why am I comfortable?

I'm comfortable because I've built up my Spiritual Fitness over time, through hard work and prayer. I'm comfortable because I've worked hard at all of the things God wants me to work toward, including overcoming my sinful nature and learning to be humble. I've also learned from the examples in history, in the Bible, and in my own life to trust that God can help us to get over great limitations and give us the ability to command courage in any situation.

Because of all of those things, what began as a journey recounted in Chapter 1 as "Searching for Inner Peace," finally brought me to the result of Chapter 7. Because I trust in God, I'm no longer searching, but instead actually *finding* inner peace.

Trusting Fully, from Battlefields to Parking Lots

Trusting God doesn't mean waking up every day and saying, "Lord, I turn this whole day over to you. I don't know what I'm going to do today but I'm sure you're going to show me." That sort of laziness is not rewarded. I am convinced that God wants us to work hard and pray hard, just as James Marsh told me.

That is why each night before I go to bed, I pull out a notebook and list the things I hope to achieve the next day. There is always work to be done, and I like to be organized about how I do it. But I do so with the full realization that whatever I write down is probably not going to happen the way I expect it to, because something is going to come up that will get in the way or completely alter my well-organized plans. And that's okay!

When those circumstances that are beyond my control come up, the first thing I do is let go and let God. I pause and think about it, and pray about it.

I did that when the Surge was announced in 2007, and I had to move 25,000 men to an unexpected destination with only six weeks of prep time. I prayed, and He showed me the way. And we accomplished our goals in Iraq.

I did that when I worked at the Pentagon and the powers that be told me I needed to trim $5 billion (yes, *billion*!) from my budget in a single year. I prayed, and He showed me how to go about making those cuts—which was not easy but did get done. (Both of those difficult endeavors are described in detail in my book, *Adapt or Die*.)

I pray and "let go, let God" in smaller situations, too. It's truly an everyday thing.

When I park my car in a parking lot, if I get a sense I should park in this spot and not that spot, that's where I park. And although some of you might laugh at me for this, I'm just gonna go ahead and admit it: I believe somehow God is telling me, "No, don't park in that place, park in this place," so I follow that command. I don't know whether that's really God telling me where to park or whether it's just me taking my beliefs to the extreme, but I find myself routinely parking where I think God wants me to park. Maybe that's weird, but it's where I'm at.

I'm convinced that God gets involved in all aspects of His children's lives. I'm absolutely convinced of that. I'm convinced that God gets involved in where you should park the car so you don't have an accident on the way out or have some dirt-bag rob you while you're unlocking the door.

We're told with God, all things are possible, which means that nothing is too big for God to handle, right? Well, I'm also convinced that nothing is too *small* for God to handle, and that includes parking lot duties.

My son-in-law David was getting ready to go out on a job interview one day while I was working on this book, and though he was nervous about it at the same time he wasn't sure it was a job he really wanted. He wasn't sure whether or not he wanted to stay put in the town he was in, or to move down to where Sarah and I were moving, which would mean his wife, our daughter, would be closer to her whole family. So we gathered our hands and prayed and asked God to be with us, and to be with David as he did his interview, and to show him the way.

David didn't get the job.

The hard part about living the Faith of the Centurion is something I mentioned earlier in this book: coming to realize that God answers all prayers, but sometimes the answer is "no," and sometimes the answer is, "not now."

When you pray for something, it doesn't always go the way you want it to go. The thing that the Bible assures us of is if you believe in God, then you believe He's got your back. You have to believe God sees a big picture that you cannot possibly see from your position in the middle of your life at this moment.

A few months later, we were loading up a trailer with my daughter's and David's things. They were making their move, and David was happy about it. He was glad he didn't get that job. Our whole family was about to be in closer proximity than we'd been since the kids were little. Hopefully that's a very good thing. I know that I, for one, am thankful David didn't get a job that would have kept them in a whole different part of Texas. And I've thanked God for His guidance in that matter.

That's a quick, easy, obvious scenario where God's decision turned out for the best. I think we see those all the time: the job you didn't get leads to the dream job you really wanted; the girlfriend or boyfriend who broke up with you leads you to find someone new, which turns out to be the relationship of your dreams. We all know these sorts of stories. We recognize them, and I believe they are proof of God's work.

But sometimes God puts you in situations that are extremely difficult and He expects you to work your way out of the situation, and that is something that is much, much harder to understand.

Romans 5:3 says:

> Not only so, but we also glory in our sufferings, because we know that suffering produces perseverance; perseverance, character; and character, hope. And hope does not put us to shame, because God's love has been poured out into our hearts through the Holy Spirit, who has been given to us.

This is hard for people to digest. It's hard for *me* to digest. Do you glory in your sufferings? Are you ever glad you are suffering? For me, the answer is still, "No!" I don't glory when I'm suffering. When something terrible happens, I don't turn to God and say, "Man, I'm glad you did that." But this is Paul saying, again, that God wants us to trust that He has our best interest at heart, He's looking at the big picture, that whatever's happening—no matter how awful it is—is God's will.

Now, in retrospect, sometimes we can look back on things and see how they lead to something better, or taught us a lesson, or made us stronger. There are lots of people who've been through tough times—maybe a divorce, or a big struggle after a job loss—and come out the other side of it better people in the end. I think there's merit in that. I think that's a positive thing we can all do, to find the silver linings. But to actually revel in the suffering while it's happening?

I ain't there yet.

Living the Faith of the Centurion is an action, not a destination. It's a work in progress, always, and this idea of glorying in sufferings is one area where I'm still working on it for sure. Although I can see how it would be nice to be able to appreciate suffering rather than suffer so much, it just doesn't feel right to me. So I struggle with it, and I take solace in the fact that I think most Christians struggle with it, deeply.

Back when I was a brigade-level commander in charge of 2,500 soldiers at Fort Hood, Texas, one of my close staff members and his wife had a baby. They were so happy about this healthy baby boy who had come into their lives, and every one of us who knew them were happy for them too.

Seven days after that baby came into the world, he died. There was no reason for it. It happened with no warning. The doctors said it was Sudden Infant Death Syndrome (SIDS), and there was nothing anybody could have done about it.

They were devastated. We all were. The tragedy permeated the entire staff. Sarah and I kept crying about it. Everybody was crying. We went over to their house and tried to console them, and what you don't ever do in situations like that is tell people, "I know what you're going through." You just don't. The fact is, you don't know what they're going through, even if you've had something similar happen in your life.

But that Sunday, my brigade chaplain stood up in front of the congregation and said something much worse. Using the above verse from Romans, he said, essentially, "It's a *good* thing that the baby died." He talked about perseverance building character, and God's got a plan, and we have to accept the fact their baby died for a reason. And the husband and wife were sitting right there in the front row. It was awful. It was not what they wanted to hear, nor what any of us wanted or needed to hear.

I don't know why God would take a baby at seven days, and I certainly wasn't about to "glory" in the suffering because it "produces character, and character produces hope." I couldn't then, and I'm still not there now.

I've watched a couple of good female friends die of cancer over the years, and I've done my best to console and counsel their devastated husbands, but I would never, ever tell them to think about it as a "good thing." I just can't imagine how anyone could do that, or say that, or even think that.

I am able to feel that those who died are in a better place. In cases where they were suffering in constant pain, I am able to understand that in heaven, their pain is gone. There is comfort in that. There is comfort in sharing that with their loved ones.

I am also able to see how life goes on after tragedies like cancer or the death of a child. The officer who lost the baby did very well in the Army. He didn't just stop; he carried on with his life, and he and his wife had additional children.

I am also able to see that sometimes, God steps in and heals the sick. There are many examples in the Bible of God healing the leper, or giving sight to the blind. There was a case at Fort Hood where one of my soldiers got into a terrible motorcycle accident. The doctors all said he was going to die. But he didn't. Not only did he not die, but he's up walking around just fine to this day.

What I can't see is the reason behind any of it. I cannot tell why God heals this person but not that one. I cannot understand why God allows the suffering of some people, and lifts others out of suffering in no time at all.

After all of my time spent on and off the battlefield, I think it's pretty clear that doctors treat, but God heals. And why God heals some but not others, even when they're good people, even when they're doing their best to live life the way God tells us to, makes no sense to me.

Why was the soldier on the motorcycle saved when James Marsh was taken? Please don't go telling me it's because God wanted a good soldier at His side. That's over-simplifying things, and in some ways it's disrespectful to all of the good soldiers who are still here with us. Are you saying that those soldiers aren't good enough for God? That's just wrong.

I think you can feel the anxiety I have over all of this. I know you've felt it yourself, in your own life, through the loss of friends or family members or even perfect strangers you've heard about on the news—the children and the innocent, the good people who were taken from us way too soon.

Well, guess what? Getting all wrapped up in the anxiety of the *whys* isn't what we're supposed to do. According to the Bible we're instructed to *not* be anxious, about *anything*—including unexpected deaths. And if we let go of the anxiety, the Bible says, if we trust that God knows what he's doing and that we can't possibly understand His infinite wisdom, we will then enjoy God's peace.

It's all spelled out right there in Philippians 4:6-7, with the line that reads, *"the peace of God, which transcends all understanding, will guard your hearts and your minds in Christ Jesus."*

The peace of God "transcends all understanding." It's beyond our comprehension. It's so much bigger than us that we just have to trust in it in order to enjoy it.

That's the way God works, as described in 1 Peter 1:8:

> Though you have not seen him, you love him; and even though you do not see him now, you believe in him and are filled with an inexpressible and glorious joy.

When I think back to the death of my grandfather, which happened before I was baptized, I remember it took me a long time to break free of the sadness. It seemed to consume me. I felt like I was dealing with it all by myself, because I was. I didn't actively seek out God's guidance. Years later, after I was baptized and after spending a number of years working on my

Spiritual Fitness, my mother passed away, and I found I was much better equipped to handle the loss. She was my mother; my greatest mentor and role model in so many ways; the woman who gave birth to me. Yet I knew she was in heaven, and I knew there was peace in that. I knew I had God with me, helping me through that storm, and I felt a sense of inner peace because of it.

I've felt that peace in the aftermath of the atrocities of war, even though I questioned why God took so many of our soldiers in the fight. I felt that peace in the days after James Marsh was taken so suddenly, even though I questioned why God would do such a thing. I've managed to feel that peace after some of the school shootings and terrorist attacks that have plagued our nation and the world so frequently in recent years.

Most recently, I felt that peace after my dad died too.

As I moved along my Christian walk, I even felt that peace about the Carrollton Bus Crash. That terrible accident which resulted in the deaths of twenty-seven people, mostly kids, which I talked about in Chapter 1, had ripple effects for years—but, it turns out, some of those ripple effects were positive. The parents of some of the kids on board became activists with Mothers Against Drunk Driving (MADD); one of them even became the organization's national president. Together, they were able to instigate changes and awareness campaigns that would save countless lives. Some of the survivors ended up leading powerful, inspirational lives, which were discussed in a 2013 documentary about the crash and its aftermath, entitled, *Impact: After the Crash*. There were sweeping changes made to bus safety rules and regulations, including adding multiple exits, pop-out windows, and wider aisles to most buses, and making it standard practice to run buses on diesel rather than gasoline. All in all, some astounding, positive changes in our world came about because of that one tragedy.

But those are *my* silver linings. Those are what we humans can see as silver linings. Those silver linings make us feel better, and yet I know not one parent who lost a child on that bus wouldn't trade all of it just to have one more day with their son or daughter. And I cannot say the good things that came from that crash were the *reason* God let that crash happen. The answer is: I don't know why God allowed that. Only God knows. And as a man who strives to live the life of the Centurion, I have to be okay with that. I have to be okay with the knowledge that my finite mind cannot understand God's actions because God is infinite. And while not knowing can be the cause of a lot of anxiety in a life without God, there's something pretty amazing that happens when you have faith: Not knowing what God's intentions are, but trusting that those intentions are good, brings you peace.

After all I've seen, all I've read, all I've learned and all I've experienced, I am convinced that the peace of God, which I cannot understand, but which I feel, is powerful enough to get us through anything.

And so, I do not worry.

I am able to live how we're told to live in Matthew 6:34:

> Therefore do not worry about tomorrow, for tomorrow will worry about itself. Each day has enough trouble of its own.

I am able to walk out of my house every morning without fear, knowing I'm wearing an armor of faith, like the one described in Ephesians 6:11:

> Put on the full armor of God, so that you can take your stand against the devil's schemes.

Just having access to that armor, all by itself, is a powerful improvement to life. Having the ability to live without fear and anxiety has made my life stunningly better than the one I led before I had that armor to wear.

But there's something else. There's something *more*.

Once we are able to do that, once we are truly able to put our trust in God, that is when God truly puts His trust in *us*.

Expanding Your Territory

In Chapter 4, I spoke about the Prayer of Jabez and the notion that when asked through prayer, God will gladly "expand your territory," giving you new roles in life, bigger responsibilities, and more work to do in His good name.

The thing I've found is that this theme shows up again and again for the faithful. Once you put your trust in God, God will take you places you never even imagined; places where you will find happiness the likes of which you've never known.

This promise is laid out in Matthew 25:21:

> "His master replied, 'Well done, good and faithful servant! You have been faithful with a few things; I will put you in charge of many things. Come and share your master's happiness!'"

Once you show your trust in God, God will share not just any happiness with you, but *His* happiness with you. There are all kinds of self-help books on the shelves today, and as I noted in the introduction to this book, I've read a whole lot of them. There's a lot of fluffy talk in Internet memes about happiness and unlocking the secrets to happiness, too. Yet none of those things seem to deliver on their promises, do they?

Maybe what's really missing in the quest for happiness is an acknowledgement that the best kind of contentment there is is one that's given by God. Because I recognize that my life is exponentially better today than it was before I put my full faith in Him. Exponentially. Living without anxiety and worry alone is a gigantic improvement. To go back to a metaphor that came up earlier in this book, I am able to sleep comfortably in my boat, knowing God is in charge, and has the ability to calm the storms all around me.

But the gifts that seem to keep coming as I continue to do God's work and share His message are beyond anything I ever dreamed, and I am certainly not the first person to experience these sorts of blessings after dedicating my life to the Lord. Which brings us back to another Biblical story involving a boat.

This story involves Jesus' disciples, after they had witnessed Jesus walking on water. In Matthew 14:29-30:

> "Come," he said.
>
> Then Peter got down out of the boat, walked on the water and came toward Jesus. But when he saw the wind, he was afraid and, beginning to sink, cried out, "Lord, save me!"

Peter let his fear get the best of him in that situation, even though he saw for himself that he was able to get out of the boat and walk on water at Jesus' behest. The eleven other disciples in the boat didn't even try to get out. They were afraid, had doubts, and felt safer just staying in the boat.

This speaks to the essence of trust in God. If you trust in God, he'll take you places you have never been before; to seemingly impossible places, even.

And what the Bible tells us is there are rewards for showing that trust. An example of this is found in the story of Abraham leaving Haran, in Hebrews 11:8:

> By faith Abraham when called to a place he would later receive as his inheritance obeyed and went, even though he did not know where he was going.

Even though he didn't know where he was going, Abraham followed the calling of God. As a result, he wound up in a place that would become his inheritance—the Promised Land.

By putting his faith in action, Abraham basked in an inheritance like no other. By putting his faith in action, Peter walked on water.

By putting our faith in action, we receive great gifts, too. By putting our faith in action, we are able to experience things that are beyond the comprehension of our human minds.

Angels Among Us

One of the gifts that comes from trusting in God is having the ability to see His work all around.

Early in my Christian walk, I thought I was doing something wrong because I didn't hear the voice of God speak to me. I heard people talk about receiving the word of God, and the advice of God, and I truly thought I was missing something because I wasn't hearing those things.

Over time, it dawned on me that God speaks to us in all sorts of ways. I believe God speaks to me through the advice and counsel I get from my personal Barnabas, Sarah. I believe God also speaks to me through other mentors and assistants who help guide us through life. When little coincidences happen, when we stumble across something that gives us an answer we've been seeking: That's the voice of God.

The more I stopped worrying about everything, the more I traded in my anxiety and put my true faith and trust in God, the more I started to see that God's been talking to me all along!

There are those who believe that there are angels among us, and when you're open to the idea of it, it seems to me that almost everyone you know has some story of a time when an angel (whether disguised as a human, or in a more ethereal form) stepped in to assist them in life. There's the proverbial story of the stranger who pulls you back from the curb when you're about to step out in front of an oncoming bus. There are stories of perfect strangers who assist people in time of need, or in times of crisis. Sarah's mother, Myrtle, had a very distinct encounter after Sarah's father died. She was driving near our military base after a harsh rainstorm, and the roads were slick. She was just about to come around a sharp corner on a particularly slick stretch of road that was covered with mud, since our tanks had been out there on a training run that morning. Just as clear as day, she heard the voice of her deceased husband say to her, "Myrtle, slow down." She listened. She slowed down. And just around that corner was a tank stalled out in the middle of the road. If she had been traveling at the speed limit, she would have slid in the mud and crashed directly into that immovable machine. Myrtle had absolutely no doubt that her husband, in the form of an angel, saved her life that day. And Sarah and I have no doubt either.

If it wasn't for my trust in God, my daily Bible study and Spiritual Fitness work, and the experiences I've seen with my own eyes, I might brush a story like that off as something that simply isn't believable. It's easy to be skeptical of these sorts of things. For many people, it takes a whole lot of hard work and prayer to get to a point where these sorts of angel stories seem remotely plausible.

Frankly, I find believing that story a whole lot easier than not believing it. I can't imagine going through life now thinking that there *aren't* angels among us. I like the idea that there are helpers looking out for us, all the time.

There's peace in that.

And, there's evidence in the Bible, in Hebrews 13:2:

> Do not forget to show hospitality to strangers, for by so doing some people have shown hospitality to angels without knowing it.

There's talk about angels in Genesis, too. In the story of Daniel, God's angel comes and shuts the lion's mouth. In Exodus there are angels who help carry out God's plans.

With trust in God, it is easy to trust that these angels are real, whether you see them with your own eyes, or not.

And when it comes to faith, it is the very thing that is unseen that is most important. As it says in Corinthians 4:18:

> So we fix our eyes not on what is seen, but on what is unseen, since what is seen is temporary, but what is unseen is eternal.

God is eternal. God is infinite. He exists far beyond the outer reaches of your understanding.

When you finally arrive at a true trust in that infinite God—after working hard and praying hard to establish that trust, and putting your faith in action—you will inevitably find you're able to do things that once seemed "impossible." You'll find you can walk through the storms, whether tornadoes in Texas or a hailstorm of bullets in Iraq, without fear. You'll find you can face obstacles in life without doubt, or worry. You'll find that you're able to bounce back from life's twists and turns, and even life's greatest hardships. You'll find that you're able to overcome your sinful nature in ways that once seemed impossible, too.

Want proof?

Just go back and read this book again, for starters. Go read the Bible. Go read the history of the great military leaders I've mentioned in these pages. Look to history for examples of those who've achieved greatness while doing God's work.

The proof is everywhere.

The upside of taking a *Work Hard, Pray Hard*-approach to life is that your life will get better. I've seen it. I've felt it.

I've studied it. And I've learned it. And now, I'm doing the work of sharing it with you.

I know that I am just a humble servant. I say all of this knowing that God is above me, and I hope I am delivering the message He wants me to share with you in the best way possible. I bow down as I deliver all of this to you—just as the Centurion bowed before Jesus, and asked him to heal his soldier.

I hope you hear it. I hope you want it. I hope you'll attempt to live life like the Centurion, too.

After all, we're all God's children. And at the end of this life, whenever that end shall come, I want to know I've done all I can to live the best life possible. For myself, and for you, what I truly hope is that whenever your day comes, you'll be able to say these words from 2 Timothy 4:7:

> I have fought the good fight, I have finished the race, I have kept the faith.